ENSLAVED

TRUE STORIES OF MODERN DAY SLAVERY

Edited by Jesse Sage and Liora Kasten

Foreword by Gloria Steinem

ISBN-13: 978-1-4039-7493-8 paperback

Library of Congress Cataloging-in-Publication Data
Enslaved : true stories of modern day slavery / edited by Jesse Sage and
Liora Kasten ; foreword by Gloria Steinem.
     p.   cm.
   Includes bibliographical references and index.

   1. Slavery—Case studies.   2. Forced labor—Case studies.   3.
Prostitution—Case studies.   4. Slaves—Biography.   I. Sage, Jesse.
II. Kasten, Liora.
HT857.E67   2006
306.3'62—dc22

                                                            2006049461

A catalogue record of the book is available from the British Library.

Design by Letra Libre, Inc.

D 10   9   8

Transferred to Digital Printing in 2014

CONTENTS

Acknowledgments   vi

Foreword
    Gloria Steinem   ix

Introduction
Behind the Stories: Modern Day Slavery in Context
    Jesse Sage and Liora Kasten   1

Chapter One
The Journey of an Orphan: In and Out of Bondage from
Haiti to Connecticut
    Micheline Slattery   11

Chapter Two
Beyond Abeeda: Surviving Ten Years of Slavery in Sudan
    Abuk Bak   39

Chapter Three
My Life as a Slave in America
    Jill Leighton   61

Chapter Four
Trapped on the Balcony: A Tale of a Sri Lankan
Held Hostage in Lebanon
    Beatrice Fernando   81

Chapter Five
Laogai: Inside China's Forgotten Labor Camps
    Harry Wu   113

Chapter Six
Out of Egypt: A Lifeline via Email for an
Enslaved Au Pair in Cairo
    Selina Juma   143

Chapter Seven
Atop the Second Wave: Testimony from a
Belarus Prison
    Sveta   163

Chapter Eight
Amazing Grace: A Slave Owner's
Awakening in Mauritania
    Abdel Nasser Ould Yessa   177

Epilogue
Where You Come In
    Jesse Sage and Liora Kasten   207

Contributors   215
Discussion Guide   217

Seven pages of photos appear between pages 112 and 113.

To all still enslaved today around the world
To all who have suffered slavery's sting

and

to Rina's granddaughter

ACKNOWLEDGMENTS

A ssembling this anthology was very much a group effort, and we want to recognize the many individuals who helped along the way.

Stephen Steinlight first suggested the idea of reviving, in the twenty-first century, the genre of the nineteenth-century slave narrative. We are grateful for the guidance and inspiration he provided. Loui Itoh, a dynamic student intern, played a central role in preparing the book proposal, negotiating with publishers, identifying potential contributors, and editing drafts. Without Loui's determination, this book would have remained a mere concept. Laura Murphy, another dedicated intern, drove the project to completion. Laura provided critical logistical support, keeping contributors, amanuenses, and editors on track. She also helped edit every chapter in the anthology and offered important insight as a student of nineteenth-century African American literature.

A core group of volunteer amanuenses helped polish the raw testimony of several survivors, spending hours interviewing, writing, and editing. Rebecca Hansen worked on several chapters, most notably the narrative of Abuk Bak.

Avi Steinberg guided Selina Juma, despite the difficulties of coordinating via weak Internet and phone connections between Boston and Kenya. Kayla Rosen helped polish many of the chapters, including a masterful edit of Sveta's narrative.

Our thanks also to William Novak and Jesse Kellerman for their work on the narrative of Abdel Nasser Ould Yessa, and to Nasira Haque, Tawny Powell, and Lillian O'Donnell for their assistance on several pieces. Diane Nguyen also provided support and insights during the editing process. Ellen Tacher helped rescue Selina Juma and graciously allowed her emails documenting the ordeal to be printed. Tacher was assisted by Hossam Bahgat of the Cairo-based Egyptian Initiative for Personal Rights, who at great risk stands up for the inherent civil rights of all people in Egypt, including trafficking victims. Wendy Lu McGill and Olga Musatovova of the International Organization for Migration in the Ukraine gathered testimony from several survivors, contributing many hours to the project. We salute their important work and thank them for the hours of assistance they provided. Stella and Valeria, two survivors who work with IOM, graciously provided personal narratives as well. Amy Reger at the Laogai Foundation in Washington, DC, guided the process of preparing Harry Wu's contribution to the anthology. Nasser Weddady of S.O.S. Slaves helped coordinate final production of Abdel Nasser Ould Yessa's chapter.

Several individuals helped us navigate the arcane world of publishing. William Hulsey offered valuable legal advice, while Brian Hotchkiss and Chip Rossetti provided much-needed advice and valuable contacts. We have of course benefited from the encouragement and careful editing of Gabriella Pearce and Alan Bradshaw at Palgrave Macmillan.

Ella's enthusiasm for the anthology project was infectious and Alan's insights were invaluable. We are so grateful to them and the rest of the Palgrave team—as well as for the continuing guidance of George Witte at St. Martin's Press.

Gloria Steinem has been a long-time supporter of the American Anti-Slavery Group, ever since she hosted Abdel Nasser Ould Yessa for tea in 2001. She kindly agreed to pen the anthology's foreword and also provided valuable suggestions throughout the editing process.

Supporting our efforts throughout have been the staff and board of the American Anti-Slavery Group. Dr. Charles Jacobs, the organization's chairman and co-founder, has inspired us with his intense dedication to the abolitionist cause and collaborated with us in writing the epilogue.

Most of all, we sincerely thank the contributors to the anthology, the slavery survivors themselves, for their tremendous courage and dedication to the anti-slavery movement. Their remarkable ability to rise out of slavery and derive strength from their experiences, becoming activists and leaders, provides the backbone of the American Anti-Slavery Group and the modern abolitionist movement.

Finally, we wish to thank the thousands of members of the American Anti-Slavery Group. As a small non-profit, we rely on donor contributions to propel our work. If you are already a supporter, we hope you will consider this anthology as your own—it could not have come together without your contribution. If you are not yet a member, we encourage you to visit www.iAbolish.org and join us today.

FOREWORD

by Gloria Steinem

"We must save the executioner from being the executioner as well as the victim from being the victim."

—Cesar Chavez

In the long struggle against the idea that one human being can own another, we have reached a dangerous stage: a time of believing that slavery is over.

Even the word "slavery"—once made so serious by centuries of slave rebellions and abolitionism that no one could use it lightly—has become a meaningless metaphor of everyday life. We say "wage slave" when we just mean a lack of capital, or "sex slave" as if it were ever about mutual pleasure, or "slave to fashion" as a testimony to cheerful consumerism.

In wealthy nations like the United States, we may see occasional television exposés of undocumented immigrants forced to work for no pay at guarded sweatshops in our cities, yet our responses still have the blame-the-victim quality of, "Why don't they escape?" *After all, slavery ended in the nineteenth century.*

We may read about Midwestern farm girls found chained to beds in Times Square or Tokyo, but our understanding of the Stockholm Syndrome is more likely to focus on intellectual political prisoners than young females whose will to survive is sapped by human traffickers adept at luring them with false promises, then "seasoning" them until they are convinced that no one will ever accept them again. *After all, slavery ended in the nineteenth century.*

In developing countries, we see the abduction and auction of child slave laborers, families trapped in debt-bondage toiling in fields, phony "adoptions" of poor children, false promises of good jobs used to lure and enslave domestic labor across borders, and even the use of the enslaved as sources of organs to be sold in a burgeoning black market. Yet many people vulnerable to these dangers continue to avert their eyes, if only because the need to survive leads to denial. *After all, how could slavery exist in the same world with modern police and the United Nations?*

That's why the personal stories in these pages are so important. Just as nineteenth-century slave narratives forced readers to recognize the humanity of slaves, these twenty-first-century slave narratives force us to recognize the reality of slavery.

Even by the strictest definition, slavery's soul-murder and slow death are facts of daily life for millions of people. If we were to include such categories as young boys forced to kill as child soldiers, or women in refugee camps seized by raiders, or indigenous Bushmen of Southern Africa used as slave labor by Bantu and white farmers alike, the numbers would become so large that involuntary servitude would form a subculture on which much of the world rests. And perhaps it does.

Yes, most forms of slavery are now illegal, at least on paper. But some cultures normalize them by caste or debt servitude or sexual practice; others create laws but do not enforce them; many pay or supervise officials so poorly that bribery becomes a way of life; and most of the enslaved themselves are too dependent, invisible, or fearful of reprisal to speak—even supposing they would be listened to.

Far out-weighing a flimsy enforcement system are the huge profits to be made from captive labor of all kinds. Profits in human trafficking are estimated to outstrip illegal arms trafficking, an industry that is easier to identify and more likely to be prosecuted. In fields peopled by laborers from the global south, child and adult slaves often cost less to acquire than farm animals. In cities, maintaining sexual servitude may cost less than other tourist attractions.

No country is safe from this river of human chattel that flows through factories and sweatshops, kitchens and crop-picking fields, red light districts and brothel beds where cruelty and humiliation are excused as male sexual needs.

In the past, the global slave trade was justified by a belief that some human beings were lower life forms, thus could and even should be owned and protected by the more evolved. These popular and respected arguments were grounded in everything from the right to private property to the pseudo-science of craniology and the slavery references in the Bible and Koran.

Now, the enslavement of many more human beings is justified by the argument that subsistence is better than nothing; or by generations of slavery that make it seem inevitable; or by the notion that sex traffickers are just "facilitating migration" for women who have "chosen" to do a kind of "sex work" from which only pimps profit; or, in the case of children, by the excuse that their families would have been unable to support them anyway. And then there are the dictators who promote or tolerate slavery without fear of being held accountable.

We can begin to see through the justifications if we use empathy. Even minor changes in language affect consciousness, as when we are careful to speak of "prostituted women and children" instead of labeling them "prostitutes," or when we make the process visible by saying "people who have been trafficked or enslaved."

We can undermine the system of slavery itself by refusing to buy goods whose provenance we don't know; by supporting strong laws that target the slave trade and those who profit from the prostitution of others; by prosecuting even well-to-do and respectable customers who patronize sex slaves; by becoming aware of and willing to report the cyber-auctioning of human beings on the Internet; by spotlighting the sex industry role played by U.S. military bases, United Nations peace-keepers, and tourist agencies; by challenging the dictators who use slavery as a means for control and ethnic cleansing; by supporting anti-slavery activists working in the face of government repression; by offering escape and safe haven to those who have been enslaved; by refusing to excuse slavery in the name of "cultural relativism"; by following our sense of empathy to what free will really means—and so much more.

But first, we must learn to recognize slavery when we see it. Just as we didn't understand the prevalence of child abuse or sexual assault until we listened to people who had survived it and learned to recognize its patterns, so too we will learn to recognize the patterns of slavery.

Listen to the voices of these survivors. They came from the darkness to bring us light. It's up to us to open our eyes.

BEHIND THE STORIES

MODERN DAY SLAVERY IN CONTEXT

Jesse Sage and Liora Kasten

In 1856, just five years before the outbreak of the Civil War, Boston abolitionist Benjamin Drew published an anthology of narratives from African American slaves who had escaped to Canada. Titled *The Refugee: Narratives of Fugitive Slaves in Canada Related by Themselves,* the book featured testimony of slavery survivors who recounted their ordeals in brutal detail.

Drew's work was one of many slave narratives published in the United States during the eighteenth and nineteenth centuries. Driven by the popularity of *The Narrative of the Life of Frederick Douglass* (also published in Boston) and Harriet Jacobs's *Incidents in the Life of a Slave Girl,* the slave narrative became a distinct genre in American literature. These first-person testimonies compelled Americans to confront the human experience underlying the political debate over slavery. Moreover, as the cases of Douglass and Jacobs attest, slave narratives produced icons for the anti-slavery movement, spotlighting individuals who came to represent the larger cause.

With the exception of the Works Progress Administration's Federal Writer's Project (WPA-FWP), which collected and edited over two thousand American slave narratives in the 1930s, the genre of slave narratives largely died out at the end of the nineteenth century. Unfortunately, we are compelled to revive it today at the dawn of the twenty-first century. Slavery persists, and survivors of human bondage must once again share their stories to awaken the public. As abolitionists working in Benjamin Drew's hometown of Boston, we have come to know many survivors of modern-day slavery. Several of these individuals have bravely agreed to recount their stories in the pages that follow. Like Douglass and Jacobs before them, they write on behalf of millions of others who remain silenced in slavery.

CONTEMPORARY SLAVERY

We do not invoke the term "slavery" as a metaphoric concept. The individuals victimized by modern-day slavery do not just have tough jobs or demanding bosses. They are not simply underage laborers or sweatshop workers. They are forced to work for no pay under the threat of violence.

Unlike the forms it assumed in past centuries, slavery today almost never involves the legal buying and selling of individuals. The moral argument against slavery has been definitively settled. No group stands up at the United Nations declaring slavery an integral part of its cultural or social identity. Every country in the world has legal codes officially outlawing human bondage. Nonetheless, millions of people—between 15 and 30 million, by various estimates—are today held as slaves. Many are women and children, society's most vulnerable members.

Contemporary slavery assumes several forms, including chattel slavery, debt bondage, sex slavery, and forced labor. Chattel (from the French word for "cattle") slaves are considered their master's property and can be bought, sold, traded, and even inherited from generation to generation. This is the form of slavery most familiar from American history, though it remains only in a few pockets around the world today. In the northwest African country of Mauritania, for instance, black Africans make up an inherited slave caste known as *haratines* who serve their Arabo-Berber masters in a socially sanctioned form of chattel slavery. Although not all Mauritanian black Africans are *haratines*, estimates put the number of slaves at over half a million.

In East Asian countries like Pakistan and India, men and women young and old work as slaves in a system of debt bondage in which they remain held as collateral against a debt they or a relative owes. The debtor is forced to work to pay off the loan, which accrues interest at an astronomical rate, as well as "repay" the costs of housing and food. The debt continues to accumulate over many years and can even be inherited by the debtor's children. A human being can thus be born into servitude and die in servitude.

Sex slavery ensnares millions of women and girls, some as young as four (young men and boys are also victims). These individuals are often kidnapped, deceived by the promise of legitimate jobs, or even enticed to work as prostitutes—only to find themselves coerced to work without pay and denied the freedom to leave or choose their clients. Some slaves in Thailand, home to a booming sex tourism industry, report being forced to service as many as 40 men a day. When illness strikes sex slaves, often as a result of forced abortion or sexually transmitted diseases, brothel owners throw them out on the street with no money or means to survive.

This collection includes stories from survivors of various forms of forced labor, including several examples of domestic slavery, in which individuals are held hostage in homes as unpaid maids. As the anthology's testimony reveals, the terrifying journey into slavery often involves leaving home, crossing borders, and encountering unfamiliar situations where escape appears impossible. Indeed, contemporary human trafficking (a term used to refer to the modern-day slave trade) is a thriving international trade, a dark underworld in today's global economy.

Economic, political, and social factors all contribute to the strength of today's system of human trafficking, now estimated to be the second-largest international crime. (The slave trade is even more developed than illicit arms sales and exceeded only by the trafficking of drugs.) Economically, slavery pays big dividends. Trafficking humans demands from the traffickers a relatively low price for the "product" and offers the enormously valuable benefit of endless free labor. For instance, brothel owners not only collect every dime earned by their sex slaves, but also pay only minimal overhead costs for substandard food, shelter, clothing, and occasional medical services.

In other cases, dictatorships tacitly endorse slavery. Burma, China, Mauritania, and Sudan are just some of the countries where the ruling regime has in various ways supported the enslavement of its own citizens. Harry Wu, Abuk Bak, and Abdel Nasser Ould Yessa provide first-hand accounts of how repressive societies can go so far as to promote human bondage. Some, like China's massive laogai forced labor camps, draw their inspiration from modern ideologies. Others invoke atavistic systems, like Sudan's revival of centuries-old Arab slave raids against African civilians.

THE HUMAN EXPERIENCE

Behind the geopolitical factors and the grim statistics are millions of personal stories. Individuals become trapped in slavery, face physical and psychological abuse, and struggle to endure—hopefully long enough to taste freedom. They make choices, react to the coercion directed at them, and undergo a complex emotional journey.

The persistence of slavery, the fact that it continues to victimize millions, may seem inexplicable. "How do people allow themselves to become enslaved?" is a question we often hear. "Why don't they just refuse or run away?" The stories in this collection reveal diverse answers. Most authors had a strong sense of self at the time of their enslavement, but nonetheless could not prevent becoming trapped. Some were lured, others violently abducted, and one individual actually grew up accepting slavery as a banal institution. Many did not comprehend the risk until it was too late.

Slaveholders use physical and psychological means to prevent slaves from escaping. Their tactics include beatings, verbal barrages, and other classic forms of intimidation. Rape and starvation are not uncommon. The stories that follow describe masters who whip, stab, gag, pull out hair, and sting with electric prods. One master for ten years calls his victim nothing other than "black slave." Another brutally trains his victim to be utterly subservient to the most perverted whims. In essence, the master's goal is the dehumanization of the slave. Stripping victims of their humanity and identity becomes a vital part of the enslavement process.

It is thus all the more remarkable how the survivors included in this collection have managed to maintain their sense of self. On rare occasions, the authors let readers in on their coping mechanisms. One survivor recalls daydreaming about childhood games; another endured by thinking of a son left behind. Despite these few revealing glimpses, the survivors' extraordinary ability to endure and ultimately recover remains largely mysterious, buried under layers of trauma and unexplainable mental tenacity. The men and women whose stories are featured herein are a self-selecting group of steadfast individuals that struggled for freedom and remained hopeful through the grimmest moments of human cruelty.

A PLATFORM FOR SURVIVORS

The American Anti-Slavery Group was founded in 1994 by Dr. Charles Jacobs to unite Americans of different backgrounds and political stripes in the struggle to end modern-day slavery. At the time, the topic of contemporary human bondage was rarely explored by journalists, academics, and human rights experts (the women's rights movement's exposés of sex trafficking being a notable exception). Dr. Jacobs and the organization's co-founders had to struggle to put slavery on the agenda. Occasional reports documented the phenomenon, but few Americans were informed or motivated to take action.

For the first five years, the organization faced a steep uphill battle simply in presenting the issue to the American public. But by 1999, a number of slavery survivors from around the world now living in the United States began to come forward. The American Anti-Slavery Group soon became a platform for survivors to speak out, helping these individuals testify to Congress, receive recognition in major American media outlets, and speak to audiences across the country. The former slaves proved to be more effective advocates than "professional" experts, providing unparalleled insight into the slavery experience and, by sharing their own triumph over exploitation, inspiring Americans to act.

This anthology was born out of our work with these survivors. Abuk Bak, who shares her story of a decade of slavery in Sudan, first told her story in September 2000, when she helped lead a protest outside the United Nations over the visit of Sudanese dictator Omar Al-Bashir. Today she is a member of our organization's speakers bureau, along with Beatrice Fernando, who recounts being trafficked into domestic slavery far from her native Sri Lanka, and Micheline Slattery, who describes the trauma of being enslaved first in Haiti and then in an American suburb. Selina Juma, a young Kenyan who found herself trapped in a wealthy Cairo household, explains in her narrative the small role our organization played in helping secure her freedom.

Harry Wu, a survivor of China's *laogai* who has devoted himself to human rights activism, collaborated with our organization in protesting the policies of PetroChina, the regime's national oil company. Sveta, the young woman who provides a gripping account of life as a sex slave in Eastern Europe, was interviewed by the International Organization for Migration (IOM), a partner organization in the Ukraine. And lest readers assume that those victimized from slavery only come from foreign countries, the collection includes the harrowing mock-diary entries of Jill Leighton, a native-born American who was forced into sex slavery.

The narratives display a wide emotional range. Some survivors invite readers into their intimate ordeal, while others remain distant. Some narratives provide a "happy" ending, yet others conclude unresolved. The materials presented here by no means offer a definitive portrait of contemporary slavery. In fact, we hope this collection will inspire many more anthologies, capturing stories from additional regions and of different types of enslavement.

To be clear, the anthology does not feature straight oral testimony, but rather crafted narratives. Most of the material in the collection is the original writing of the survivors themselves. Several individuals, who are not fluent in English, worked with amanuenses to prepare their chapters (as did many of the nineteenth-century slavery survivors who published narratives). All prose has been clarified by editors, but always with the attempt to preserve the survivor's language and style.

This collection concludes with an unusual twist: the narrative of a slave owner. Abdel Nasser Ould Yessa, our colleague for over five years, is the foreign secretary of the Mauritanian anti-slavery group S.O.S. Slaves. He is also a former master, having been born into an elite clan of Mauritanian Arabo-Berbers who owned hundreds of black slaves. As Yessa recounts, he grew up surrounded by slaves, who existed to attend to his every need. His narrative describes Mauritania's unusual system of chattel slavery, but also the moment that sparked his conversion from slave owner to abolitionist.

Yessa's unusual perspective reveals the human complexity of contemporary slavery, particularly in a society in which servitude is accepted as an established institution. His narrative of personal rebellion and ethical enlightenment sheds new light on the position of the slaveholder without drawing moral equivalents between the slaveholder and the slave, as Yessa himself comes to define slavery as immoral and utterly unacceptable.

THE ROLE OF THE READER

Like the writers of nineteenth-century slave narratives, the survivors featured in this collection are quite conscious of their audience. Each seeks to connect with you, the reader, and motivate you to act.

Following the narratives, we have provided a brief epilogue to address some lingering questions, in particular about why the world has allowed slavery to flourish—and how you can contribute to the growing neo-abolitionist movement. A brief checklist outlines specific steps you can take to make a difference.

We share the following slave narratives with a mix of regret and optimism. We apologize for asking you to read such frank accounts of human cruelty and unnecessary suffering. Yet we trust that you will respond not only with disgust, but with a determination to help end slavery once and for all.

Chapter One

THE JOURNEY
OF AN ORPHAN

IN AND OUT OF BONDAGE
FROM HAITI TO CONNECTICUT

Micheline Slattery

Micheline Slattery bears few outward signs of her ordeal. Her bubbly demeanor, elegant style, and fluent English betray little hint of a brutal childhood and young adulthood. Her trauma begins with the assassination of her father in Haiti and then lasts nearly two decades, including enslavement in both Haiti and a Connecticut suburb. The excerpt below reveals a young woman who—despite appearing tragically marked for abuse—is a survivor, determined to overcome.

The type of slavery Slattery experienced is referred to in Haiti as restavec—*literally, "staying with." By some estimates, 250,000 young Haitian children today are* restavecs, *serving as domestic slaves for Haitian families. Although slavery is outlawed in Haiti, these young Haitians—sometimes even relatives of the slaveholders—are seen as expendable. They are forced to do the most menial work for no pay and often live in terrible conditions.*

Haiti was historically a massive French slave colony; hundreds of thousands of Africans were transported to the Caribbean island to work on plantations. A slave rebellion in 1804 overthrew the rule of white slave owners. Yet, the restavec *system soon emerged, as former slaves began holding young children as slaves. Today, Haitian children caught up in the* restavec *system are sometimes trafficked to the United States. Slattery's story is but one example.*

I was born on July 13, 1977, in the coastal community of Jacmel in Haiti, the second child of privileged, mixed-race parents. I was less than a year old when my father was assassinated by the *Tonton Macoute,* a ruthless gang formed to enforce submission to the Duvalier presidency then seizing power.* My parents were popular with the residents of Jacmel, and my father had a reputation for helping the people of Haiti, who desperately needed it. They were happy, as far as I know, but things changed.

---

*Francois Duvalier, president of Haiti from 1956 to 1971, was known for his corruption and despotism. The *Tonton Macoute,* a private squad he established to terrorize and assassinate perceived foes of his regime, continued to operate during his son's reign as president until he was forced to flee to France in 1986.

After my father's death, my mother, my older brother Lewis, and I went into hiding on a farm we owned in Jacmel. The farm was our playground, and we grew up in relative happiness, unaware of the dark events motivating the move. Rice, corn, and coffee were grown for export, and stretching away from the house in all directions were fields worked by silent men who would arrive before we awoke and then vanish at sundown. Our life acquired a semblance of peace, but beneath the idyllic surface was hidden a volatile situation.

My mother never quite got over my father's death. She worked hard to keep the farm going, to keep her children fed. Sometimes, in those years following my father's murder, my mother would break down at the sink or in her bedroom, weeping for my father. Her room was next to mine, and I could hear her sobbing at night. Sometimes I would leave my room and go lie next to her without saying anything. I would put my little arms around her and she would take them and kiss them, and we'd fall asleep.

The morning my mother left me began like any other. My brother ran off to play with friends, and after spending the morning running around in the bushes near the house, I retreated inside. On the carpet in the living room, I'd spread a few dolls, and above me, at a small table in the corner, my mother hunched over some paperwork. Then the three men came. They wore old clothes, perhaps from the military, and bright red kerchiefs around their necks. Each wore an expensive gold watch and rings. As soon as my mother answered the door, I knew there was going to be trouble. She looked scared as she ushered them into a sitting room and sent the maid to make tea.

I was banished to the kitchen and didn't hear what was said. Fear began to take hold of me, unlike anything I had previously felt. It was a sick, cold feeling low in my stomach. My whole body seemed chilled by it. I kicked my little legs back and forth while cooks bustled over the stove, setting water to boil. They didn't look at me. Plain white walls, and the elaborate chrome workings of the oven, which took up one whole wall, held and lost my nervous gaze.

The teapot began to shriek just as my mother came into the kitchen, and she jumped. Without a word, she took my hand and led me out of the kitchen, through the elegantly decorated rooms, and out the back door. We passed mango trees, the orange grove, the small herb garden one of the cooks kept next to the shed. Soon we had skirted a corn field, the ground torn up but the furrows yet unseeded, and entered the brush. Dense jungle wrapped around us, its stillness belying the urgency of the woman pulling me along. She assured me I was going to an aunt's, but when we reached a lake, at the foot of a dark mountain, she left me there. She told me Lewis had been sent to a friend's house for the night.

"Stay put," she told me, her voice cracking. "Your aunt will come get you. Do not move. I'll see you soon, my darling." She kissed me quickly. Then she vanished through the undergrowth. That was the last time I saw my mother. She had recognized those men as agents of the *Tonton Macoute*, the same men who had killed my father. I can only assume she met the same fate.

I lay down in the dark grass. Water was vast on all sides, and above it the mountain, tall and verdant in the heavy air. Hours passed. The sun began to sink and the call of animals soon replaced the light. Their voices pierced the deep pitch of the forest. My own panic slowly grew. There was no sign of anyone, only the veiled step of nonhuman life in the darkness. A fear came to me that I was going to die, alone. I cried and called my mother's name into the jungle. I began to walk aimlessly, stumbling forward and back, tripping and falling on my face, desperate for my mother, but there was no answer. I needed a human voice. I began to climb the mountain. Thorns grasped at my clothes. The uncertain terrain caused me to lose my balance, hitting the ground more than once. My foot was bleeding. My shirt and pants were torn and soiled. I wandered blindly, going up, up, up.

After what seemed like hours, a deep male voice began to drift toward me from above. I ran toward it, crying for help. My fear of those strange men who terrorized my mother had disappeared in my need for reassurance. I broke out of the brush and into the arms of a large, dark-skinned, old man. He seemed to be another part of the mountain; his voice was deep and thick and rumbled out of him. But his eyes were kind in the light of his torch, and I was not afraid of him. I was crying at this point, and between sobs tried to tell him what happened. He let me carry on for a minute or so, and then called to someone behind him, who came out quickly into the light. She was an old woman, heavily wrinkled, but she moved quickly, and took charge of the situation immediately. His wife took me inside, cleaned my cuts, all the while asking me who I was and where my family was. After breakfast the next morning, we descended the mountain, the woman and I. The forest seemed less frightening with an adult by my side. I was brought to my aunt's house, across town in a poorer area of Jacmel.

My aunt and her family accepted me into their lives. But as soon as the kind woman on the hill departed, I was put to work. My aunt used me as the family maid. Though I was only five years old, I was given a long list of chores that kept me busy sunrise to sunset. I was to wake up at six every morning, in the cool of dawn. I would dress quickly and rush through the mist-hung jungle, half-asleep, to fill three one-gallon buckets at the lake five miles from our home. Four or five times in one day, I would make the journey. There were no roads or even footpaths. Snakes rested on vines or hid in the thick grass underfoot.

If ever the water supply ran low, I would be whipped without mercy by my aunt, who used flexible rods designed for the purpose. I still remember the pain. Once, though I forget my transgression, I was whipped so severely by my aunt that a gash opened on my back. My aunt went inside to the kitchen, sliced up a handful of lemons, added handfuls of salt, and rubbed them into the wounds. She did all this without apology or remorse of any kind. Whenever she would whip me, I would keep my mind blank, or try to. The pain, however, soon overwhelmed my thoughts. All I could do was pray that the next stroke would be the last.

My servitude was not restricted to fetching water. My day was so full that any hesitation would mean leaving things undone. After the other children went to school, I was to make their beds, clean the house, wash the dishes, and perform all the other tasks that kept the house running. To wash the clothes, I would stuff them into a great wicker basket, which I would balance on my head as I made my way to the lake, across the same path I carried water. The clothes weighed nearly as much as the water did. Along the way my neck would begin to cramp badly, but I did not stop to rest or slow down for fear of punishment. Still, this was probably my favorite part of the day. I was away from the abusive treatment of the house, and the work was easy enough, though my hands would be an angry red by the end. This was the only real time I had to think. I would miss my mother and my father, and sometimes I would tell myself that they were coming back.

My aunt and uncle, both practicing *Voudou* priests, reputedly made a deal with *Damballah-wédo*, the snake god, during the seasonal festivities one night. They requested great wealth and power and the ability to rise above the meager livelihood of the provincial farmer that was their lot. In return, they promised the spirit the life and soul of their youngest child, whose name was Marian. Marian was my age, a beautiful, light-skinned child. The phrasing of the ritual described the union between the spirit and the child as a "marriage," and she was expected to develop a strange, inexplicable illness that would quickly take her life. Her soul would then belong to the spirit, to do with as he pleased. Over the next few years, my aunt and uncle's farm began to grow and prosper. Soon, they were among the wealthiest farmers in Jacmel and became the acquaintances of a number of influential people in Port-au-Prince and elsewhere. Then one day Marian became sick. The spirit was taking his prize, as promised. My aunt and uncle now balked at their side of the bargain, horrified at the thought of losing their beautiful girl. They knew the spirit must be paid, but they thought perhaps a different soul could be substituted for that of their daughter.

They quickly turned to me. I was then about seven years old and an unwanted child in the household, more a slave than a family member. I made a perfect sacrifice. A propitious day was chosen for the invocation, and that morning I was given my first real bath since arriving at the house. They bathed me and dried me, and I wondered at how nice my skin looked when it wasn't smudged with dirt. They wrapped me in fine white linens and silk, and draped me in long, beaded jewelry. I was dressed as a traditional Haitian bride. I glanced at myself in the mirror after they were done and didn't recognize my own reflection. I thought they were finally starting to care for me, that all my hard work had been recognized. *Finally,* I thought, *I have a family again.*

My aunt and her husband, of course, mentioned nothing about what was to come that night. They kept me in the fancy clothes all day and excused me from chores. I was given a warm meal with everyone else at the table. I was ready to head off to bed that night when my uncle came in and took my arm. "You must come with us," he said, in a strange voice. I was confused; it was late at night, but I was too afraid that they might change their opinions of me. I followed him. We went outside, and my aunt joined us, with several others. They were dressed in the robes and animal skins of the *Voudou* rites. I started to get worried. We walked for miles through the dense darkness to reach the cave where the altar was located. No one spoke.

As we approached the cave I saw a dim, flickering light coming from inside. Low voices drifted towards me as I drew nearer. I tried to turn back, but six pairs of hands clamped down on me and dragged me forward. I entered. Bones littered the upraised earth where the altar stood, and lit candles on the altar and in small niches throughout the cave provided the only light. My aunt put on her horsehair headdress, and, taking a bone in each hand, began the slow, undulating rhythms that would call the spirit to overtake her, using her body as a medium through which the spirit would communicate. I was lifted onto the altar, where I stood, ringed by black candles. I remained silent, too petrified to cry. The chanting reached a crescendo, then all of a sudden stopped. My aunt was standing in the center of the room. It was exactly midnight.

The snake god had entered my aunt. Her movements ceased to be human. She sat down like an animal, and everyone quickly kneeled before her. My uncle spoke, saying "here, take this child." They began offering me to the spirit, pleading with it to take me instead of Marian, who had been promised. My aunt had remained motionless while they pleaded, but suddenly she looked up, and her eyes had a strange emptiness in them. She looked straight at me. Then, just as suddenly, the candles expired. The cave was plunged into darkness, except for one candle that burned near my aunt, illuminating her terrible countenance. She spoke, and her voice was masculine, but twisted, and filled with anger. "She is not one of us!" the spirit roared. "I cannot take her." I began to sob and jumped off the altar and ran from the cave. Her dead eyes, that terrible voice—I had to get away, farther and farther away. I could hear my uncle's frantic pleading in the background as I fled the cave. *Even the spirits don't want me, even demons refuse to accept me,* I thought. I fell asleep beneath a mango tree, too far from my aunt and uncle's house to make it back.

For a brief time that year, I was sent to work for my cousin, Therese, who moved to Port-au-Prince, the capital. My aunt had been brutal, and my work for her was difficult, but my cousin was worse. Therese was about twenty-one, living as the mistress of a man she had met in the city. He kept an apartment for her and her nine siblings. I was expected to care for these ten people. My tasks were similar to those I performed in Jacmel: fetch water, do the dishes, keep the house clean, and also go food shopping and run errands. It was in Port-au-Prince that I learned how to do things like handle money and make my way through a city.

One evening, about a year after I arrived, Therese came home late. I heard her stumbling around, bumping into things. She was drunk, but at the time all I knew was that she was acting strange. She moved around downstairs for a while. Then she came into the room where I was lying, pretending to be asleep. She had removed her clothes. I saw the way her dark skin glistened in the moonlight coming in through the window, the thin veneer of sweat on her. The sour smell of alcohol floated into the room. She stumbled over to the bed, sat down, and shook me, but I no longer pretended to be asleep. She told me to touch her. I was frightened and refused. She became angry. She dragged me out of bed. "Do as you're told," she yelled. When I continued to resist her advances, she slapped me. Then she picked me up off the floor, carried me out of my room, and threw me down the stairs. My left shoulder was wrenched from its socket. Pain flared in my arm.

The next morning, Therese called the local healer. Even Port-au-Prince lacked modern medical facilities at this point, and the healer handled most of the injuries in the area. The healer, a very old man who seemed immortal to me, nodded solemnly and then beckoned me over. Without saying a word, his strong hands took hold of my body. One hand braced my back while the other lifted the left arm and snapped the shoulder back in with one movement. I screamed. With a nod to my cousin, he left the apartment.

The arm mended in time, but the next night, Therese came home intoxicated again, snuck into my room, and raped me.

When Therese heard I had told a neighbor, she grabbed a cooking knife off the counter, grabbed my arm, and pulled the blade across my cheek, cutting deep. As blood ran down my face, she threatened to do the same between my legs if I ever told anyone else what had happened the night before.

One day, when I was back at my aunt's house, while I was attending to my work at the river, God sent me a dream of a beautiful woman with creamy skin and long, flowing hair. She was coming to rescue me from this misery. I woke and rose, feeling at peace for the first time since I had fallen into the hands of my aunt.

I returned home, and waiting for me was the woman I had seen in my vision. The stranger saw me, and immediately peppered my aunt with questions. Who was I? Why was I so dirty? My aunt's answers were vague, and the woman seemed to be getting angrier and angrier. In tears, the woman sent a cousin to bring her a basin of water and played with my hair as she embraced me on her lap. That was the first time anyone aside from me had ever been sent for water in that house. It was also the first time anyone ever fussed over me. She undressed me and bathed me, horrified at the scars that ran the length of my body, the product of years of constant beatings. She rubbed cream on my skin and dressed me in new clothes. As she doted over me, I asked her, "Why are you crying?"

Her father had been a politician whose mulatto skin and position of power made him a target for the *Tonton Macoutes*. One day, a van came screeching up beside him, and a group of young, heavily armed *Tontons* forced him into the van at gunpoint. A few days later his body was recovered in a nearby lake, riddled with bullets. A band of *Tontons* had shown up at the family's house that night, ready to finish the job, but my father had taken the family in when no one else would and hid them during the subsequent searches. The least she could do, she said, was to take care of me.

She told my aunt I would be returning with her to Port-au-Prince. My aunt didn't dare disagree.

The woman's name was Leonie. She was a cousin of mine, and she was also the wife of a government official and therefore a very powerful woman. When we returned to her apartment in the capital, I was placed in a prestigious private school, allowed clothes, and most of all, given free time. Nannies fawned over me, and several servants took care of the chores I had once performed alone. A driver took me to school every day even though the journey was only a few blocks. While I lived in my cousin's favor, the dresses I owned were all store-bought and my room was large and beautifully decorated. Leonie would take days off from work to go shopping with me. We picked out things for my room, and then we'd go to a fancy restaurant for lunch in downtown Port-au-Prince. While Leonie was haggling over the price of crabs or testing the firmness of a tomato, I would spend my pocket money on sweets. At the end of the day, Leonie would take my hand, we'd get into the waiting car, and I'd fall asleep on the way home. When we reached the house, Leonie would quietly go into the house and send a nanny out to carry me into bed.

These days were soon over. Leonie doted on me for about a year, at the end of which she unexpectedly became pregnant. As soon as the pregnancy was confirmed, life changed. Now, the woman who had talked so convincingly about saving me from servitude, who had acted so disgusted at the poor treatment I had received, became as bad as my previous keepers. She forced me to work all the time. She even allowed her husband to mistreat me. One night, when I was asleep, he got up and came into my room. He was a big man, very dark, and the mattress sagged beneath his weight. I was frightened. Memories of Therese came back to me. I shivered when his hands started running over my body and under my nightgown. He whispered in a quiet, sing-song way. "You're such a sweet girl. I'm sorry I was mean to you." He tried to pull my nightgown up over my head, but I hugged my chest so he couldn't get it off. "It's all right," he told me, "it's all right, we're just going to play a game." But I wouldn't move my arms, so he got up and left. The next morning I told Leonie what her husband had tried the night before. She became enraged, cursing me and slapping me hard across the face. She told me I was a liar and a slut.

Leonie banished me from the main dwelling, and I was given a small cottage off to the side, abutting the tall hedges that ran the length of the house. Instead of my old, luxurious room with its high bed piled with covers and stuffed animals, I had a small cot. The stuffing stuck out like snow from the ends. The lights didn't work half of the time, so I collected some spare candles from the main house and kept a supply on the cracked oak table next to the stove. Leonie put me in a public school, far inferior to the elite private academy I had previously attended. I was forced to go straight home after school to get the housework done, and was scarcely able to gather the energy at the end of the long day to start my homework. I did well enough in school, but I often couldn't focus.

Life continued this way for a few more years, until I reached the age of fourteen, when the true source of Leonie's income was revealed to me. One day, while working, I was approached by her with an offer. She asked me if I would like to go to America. I was shocked. This woman, who had been so cruel to me, was really making me such an offer? Of course, I said, I would love to go to America. It was like the heavens had opened and invited me to come up, I remember telling her.

But then a month-long training session began. Leonie schooled me as to how to respond to the customs officers. She played the role of the officer. She instructed me to say I was visiting my brother and sister in Miami, which I then believed was the truth. She gave me a new name and passport. At first, I had trouble remembering my new identity, and my cousin would lose patience and slap me. I was still working hard in her household, and had difficulty focusing at the end of the day. But I applied myself, and soon had the information mastered. I saw it all as a sort of game, but also as evidence of the privilege that was being bestowed on me. America must be a wonderful place if I had to study so hard just to be allowed entry.

To the residents of Haiti, America was like an Atlantis, or even an El Dorado, a place where everyone was rich and happy. In our imaginations, there was work for everyone, and the government behaved itself, in direct contrast to the organized purges of the Duvalier regime then in power in Haiti. Free passage, which was what Leonie was offering, seemed too good to be true. Indeed it was—Leonie was a dealer in human labor, a trafficker of people into other countries as unpaid servants. As wife of a government official, she held the necessary influence and contacts to operate without interference from authorities. I, of course, didn't realize until many years later that I was just a pawn in Leonie's extensive enterprise.

Finally the day arrived that I would fly to America. Leonie was unusually quiet that morning as she munched on some toast and I ate a mango. When we arrived at the airport, she just said "goodbye." I can't say I was sorry to leave her, or even to leave Haiti.

In Haiti, the interview had seemed so far away that I did not worry. When I arrived in America, however, I was shaking. The customs officials in my imagination were cruel and looked for weakness, like Leonie. But the real customs official was surprisingly friendly, and he put me at ease. He asked the questions routinely, and I provided routine answers. Just like that, I became an American. I took a taxi out to Miami for the best three weeks of my life up until then.

The building my half-sister lived in was dingy, covered on the outside with graffiti. The stairs were empty, dark, and they smelled bad. I knocked on the door of my half-sister's apartment. The apartment was a mess. Kids slouched on couches, slept on the floor. Roaches ran into the corners. My half-sister appeared. She was extremely skinny. She smiled and hugged me, and then began to talk and talk. She didn't know why I had gotten lucky enough to come to America, but she was so glad I was here. She hoped I would stay for a long time, however unlikely it seemed. She never stopped talking, and I was content those first few days just to listen to her voice.

My half-sister and I grew close during those three weeks, but then Leonie showed up at the apartment unexpectedly. When she learned I hadn't made it to "my destination," a destination she had never mentioned, she became furious.

She arranged a flight for me to Connecticut. I became frantic. I did not want to leave my half-sister, or this small taste of freedom I had just experienced. Because I was unwilling to budge, Leonie sent my half-sister with me to the airport to calm me down and get me on the airplane. When we got to the airport, I pleaded with my half-sister to run away with me, to leave this circle of violence and servitude. Whatever the streets could offer, it had to be better than what I had known in Haiti. But she wouldn't go with me. It took years for me to forgive her for that reluctance to flee, and her stoic abandonment of me to my fate, of which I was ignorant and she was not.

In Connecticut, I was assigned work in the home of yet another cousin, Jocelyne, then living not far from Stamford. She and her husband lived in a one-bedroom apartment with their three children. I was told to sleep on the couch. The first morning—no sooner, it seemed, than I had drifted to sleep—someone started shaking me. I woke up to my cousin, rudely forcing me to wake up. "Come," she shouted, "it's six-thirty, you must help with the children." I did as I was told, and I was introduced to a pattern of constant work that continued for years.

I didn't know what to do at first, so I walked into the bedroom of the oldest child, Naomi. I tried to wake her. She started screaming. I backed off, but then my cousin appeared in the doorway and screamed even louder for me to get going. I tried to smile, but as I was standing there, the young girl leaned forward and bit me on the arm. Now it was my turn to scream. I jumped back, stunned, as Naomi rolled over and tried to get back to sleep. I grabbed the small child and dragged her out of bed, howling and kicking. I then went into the next room and repeated the process with their other children. They would bite and kick me, even spit on me. The children might have had Biblical names, but they were terribly spoiled and soon picked up the habit of abusing their luckless caretaker. I had no defense: their mother never corrected them when they hit me, ignored me, or spat on me, even in public. I was helpless, and they knew it. If I refused to do as my cousin demanded, she would pull and twist my ears until they bled, screaming insults at me, calling me a useless fool and an ingrate.

After two weeks of living with them, my cousin registered me for the local middle school. Each day before I was allowed to go to school, I had to see off the other kids, making sure they got on the school bus before I myself could walk to school. This meant I was always late, which was a source of constant trouble. I spent many mornings in the principal's office, trying to make excuses for my tardiness, afraid to tell the truth. They would call my house, and my cousin would tell them I was lazy, that I couldn't get up on time. This made me bitter, as I was then rising at five in the morning to get breakfast on the table, make sure everything was clean, and get the kids up and dressed in time for school.

School became increasingly difficult. This was compounded by my isolation. Every day after school I went right home to begin work, so I never had the opportunity to study, make friends, or socialize. As a result, the children at school turned against me, singling out my second-hand clothes. I had the same overalls and faded, homespun dresses I had brought with me from Haiti. I thought they were beautiful once, but I came to hate them as kids belittled them. The children's mockery made me run from them more, and this distance between me and my peers increased the feeling in me that I was less than human, that I was somehow inferior to them.

At home, I constantly attempted to have my family recognize my humanity. I once confronted my cousin about her treatment of me. I asked her, "If you hate me so much, why do you keep me?" She slapped me and yelled at me. She told me, "I own you. I paid twenty-five hundred dollars for you. If you try to run, I'll deport you." That was when I learned how much I was worth, twenty-five hundred dollars. I was terrified of what would happen if my secret was discovered. My cousin told me I would be deported, that Leonie would hurt me if I returned to Haiti. I was told she would cut my face with a machete. So I kept the secret, going to great lengths to lie for the woman.

Yet when I cooked or cleaned, what was in my head wasn't escape, but a sincere desire to do a good enough job that my cousin would notice, would commend me for something, or show appreciation. One night I was convinced I had performed my work particularly well. I had been on my knees for three hours after school scrubbing the floor. I had put the kids to bed without fuss, cleaned the dishes and put them away, and the clothes were drying neatly on lines in the bathroom. Everything was in place. Jocelyne came into the kitchen as I was admiring my work. She didn't say anything. I remember catching her eye and saying, "Can't you love me?" She looked right back at me and said, "Do I look like I could ever be your mother?" Then she walked away.

Soon after this episode was the first time I tried to kill myself. It was a frigid night in January, and outside a powerful blizzard flogged the streets and houses, filling yards with foot after foot of snow. I had just gotten out of the shower, and was faced with another night of long labor. I had never felt so alone. I stripped off my towel, stepped into a pair of shorts and a tee shirt, and began walking towards the door. My wet hair clung to the back of my neck and my bare feet were chill against the wooden floor. I reached out and unlatched the lock, turned the knob, and let the door swing wide. Cold surged into the room, and the darkness yawned before me, like the open maw of something infinitely sinister. I stepped out into the storm.

I could barely breathe. A pain quickly rose in my feet and hands, but then faded. I was ready to die. I purposely walked in the middle of the street, realizing that a car could come and strike me. But these were not coherent thoughts, only whispers from a deeply buried rationalism. I felt nothing, and even the fierce weather had trouble breaking down that barrier of numbness. I do not remember what happened that night, only that I eventually reached the highway. Apparently, I passed out by the road, and a passing motorist saw my half-frozen body and took me to a nearby hospital. Fortunately, I had not been lying down long. It took months for my fingers and toes to regain full sensation, but I was alive. Had the driver not stopped and taken me to shelter, I surely would have died on that harsh New England night.

My second attempt at taking my own life was much later. I had just seen the kids off to school, and as the school bus disappeared around a corner, I saw a car come down the road after it. Without conscious thought, I stepped in front of the vehicle. My body was struck hard and thrown onto the asphalt sidewalk. The driver screeched to a halt and jumped out of his vehicle. It was a white man, middle-aged, looking terrified. I'd given him no time to stop. Miraculously, I was completely unharmed. Not even a scratch where my hands had hit the pavement to break my fall. He ran over to me, while a neighbor rushed inside to call 911. I was furious. I stood up and began cursing in Creole. Not even death wanted me! I couldn't live, I couldn't die. There really was no escape from my servitude.

The man looked more and more worried and very uncomfortable, but unwilling to leave until he was sure I was all right. Then I heard the sirens and began to curse louder. I took off running down the street, and a police car began to follow me, tailing me home. I went into the house and started to throw things. The officer followed me in, telling me I ought to go to the hospital to get checked out. So I threw a plate at him. I think he considered arresting me, but having received no training in furious Creole women throwing dishes, and seeing as I was apparently unharmed, he hurried out of the house. The driver had followed the police cruiser, and despite obvious trepidation he boldly approached the house, probably out of curiosity at this point more than concern. He asked me in English, again, if I was all right, and I ignored him. Then he asked me where I was from. I told him Haiti. "Oh," he said, "that explains it. You must know Voodoo." I stopped my pacing and just began to laugh. I told him I did not know Voodoo, if I did I would be able to kill myself properly. His bemused expression immediately became concerned again. He asked me why I would want to do such a thing. So I began to tell him, about the work I was forced to do, about how no one seemed to care if I lived or died, how I felt so alone in the world. Now, I told him, death too has rejected me. He listened for a long time. Then he left, but before he did, he wrote down all his information, in case an injury appeared, or if I just needed to talk. I never saw him again, or took him up on his offer, but those few hours were enormously therapeutic.

When Jocelyne got home that evening, she asked, a bit worriedly, why the police had been at our house. She listened to my story, and then began striking the top of my head, calling me an idiot and a fool. She told me that in America, if a car so much as touches you, you can sue for millions of dollars. That is the American way, she said.

When I turned seventeen, I was told to find a job. Before I did that, I needed working papers, which meant another call to Florida and a fifteen-hundred-dollar fee which my cousin paid, placing me in her debt. This simple process was a major factor in my remaining with her for as many years as I did. She informed me that if I tried to run away she would call immigration and I would be deported.

After acquiring the papers, I began working as a cashier at a restaurant called Duchess. When I added the job to my workload, with its seven-hour shifts six days a week, sleep was all but cut out. I would rise at five, work until school, come home, rush off to work, return home again around midnight, and then clean, iron clothes, etc. until all my work was done, and then rise again at five. I was lucky to get an hour of sleep. My cousin told me she would keep the money I earned safe for me. In fact, I never saw that money. I was merely another breadwinner for her family.

Still, I loved having a job. I got a respite from housework and made friends. I actually liked putting on the Duchess uniform because it was clean and something new, the first new thing I had put on in years. The people I worked with were nice, the work wasn't hard, and I could find a few hours of peace before I returned to the house with its demands. When I realized that Jocelyne was never going to let me spend my own money, I opened my own account. I never handed over another check, and at the end of the week, when she asked me for my check, I told her I no longer needed her assistance in managing my money. She did not pursue the subject, and from then on I had a small but steady income which would later aid my attempts to make a life of my own.

At work, I befriended a coworker, and as we were talking one day, I mentioned a brother I was supposed to have in the country, Eli Joseph. My friend became excited and informed me that he actually knew Eli. In fact, he was in Connecticut. He had known I lived here but didn't know how to contact me. My friend arranged a meeting. We went to an expensive restaurant, and suddenly there in front of me was Eli, a brother I had never met. I made quite a scene, jumping up and down and yelling for everybody to hear. I was so excited to find someone who could really care for me, someone I could claim as blood who might actually treat me that way. He was a handsome man of twenty-three then, dressed well and looking successful. He too had been trafficked into America, but had since fled his keepers and achieved success. He had married, and was living in an apartment in Connecticut with his wife until they could move out of the state. This meeting was the beginning of the end for me in Jocelyne's house.

I decided to leave. It had taken years for me to make this decision, but what finally motivated me was an offer from my brother to live with him. I packed my things, ignoring the now feeble protests of Jocelyne. I took back my high school diploma, which she had not allowed me to keep, and accepted my brother's offer of a new life.

I was twenty years old. Money was scarce and privacy rare, but I was free to make my own decisions for the first time in my life. I suppose I felt like a college student, finally liberated, but from such an extreme repression. For the first time, I made real friends and was free to go out with them. After putting myself through nursing school with money earned as a secretary, I became a practicing nurse and got my own house in the suburbs. I dated a few guys after my escape, and even fell in love for the first time. My sister-in-law introduced me to a guy she knew. He fell in love with me fairly quickly; then he set about courting me.

He swept me off my feet, dazzling me with fancy cars and jewelry. He spent money, which I had never had at my disposal, to win me over, and was also sweet and flattering. Also, he was an important man, and that made me feel privileged to be his girlfriend. I had no reason to suspect he would turn out to be a monster and that my enslavement had not entirely come to an end.

We dated for about a year, and during that time he bought me a car and paid my rent. But soon, I began to notice an increased level of concern from him about my activities during the times I was not with him. He would ask very detailed questions about what I had done on the nights I hadn't seen him. He became upset when I wanted to visit my girlfriends, and he quickly became openly controlling. Fights began to outnumber the good times as he demanded more of my time and tried to forbid me to see the friends I'd been living with not six months ago. I moved in with him, and that's when I realized many women were calling him and that he was unfaithful. We fought and fought, and he would end most of our verbal battles by striking me. After a year, I'd had enough. I left him.

But a few months later, he called me. He apologized for the things he'd done, and told me he had changed. I believed him, foolishly, and we got back together. He treated me like a princess, and a steady stream of expensive presents kept me dazzled.

Then fate intervened. One day at home I got a call from work informing me that my working papers had expired; I would not be allowed to return to work without them. I was shocked—I didn't even know working papers *could* expire. I began calling people, and soon I called Jocelyne, the one who had procured the papers. She was scornful, and mocked my attempt at living on my own. At the end of the call she told me, sounding a bit amused, that the papers were of course fake.

I wasn't legal. I never had been legal, but this came as quite a surprise to me. Now that my fake working papers had expired, I would be deported. This filled me with fear. I was just beginning to forge a life, and now I would be sent back to a country where I would probably be enslaved yet again. When I called my boyfriend, he listened calmly and then told me things would be all right. If I wanted to stay in the country, we could get married, and then I'd be granted citizenship and get a green card. I felt forced to marry him, and the ceremony took place in Las Vegas soon after.

We went then to get an appointment with immigration to get my green card. But there was a problem. Because of his attempts to control me, I had not gotten my name on any of his accounts or properties. Legally, besides the marriage certificate, there was nothing to say we were married. The man who met with us said that we needed more proof, and another meeting was scheduled. However, the number of people seeking citizenship in this country is enormous, and we could not get another meeting for five years. In the interim, I would not be deported, but I would lose my protected status if the marriage ended, reinforcing how trapped I was. This was the beginning of a whole new type of slavery.

That night my husband's manner changed again. Like someone had flipped a switch, the sweet person I had known became the controlling one I had left a few months before. Only now, I couldn't leave him, and he knew it. "I own you," he said, "if you want to stay in this country, you do what I say."

He began to dictate what I could and could not do. He would forbid me to talk on the phone, and when the phone bill came, he would check every single number, to make sure I hadn't disobeyed him. He would beat me, but he was clever about it, and knew how to hurt me without leaving marks. Afterwards he would brag about what he had done, how smart he was to cause me so much pain without leaving evidence. For five years I lived like this. I stopped giving myself to him, and he began to rape me almost every night. He was brutal, and sometimes he'd be rough enough to draw blood.

Eventually I became pregnant. I am a Catholic, and didn't want an abortion, but he made me get one. He drove me to the clinic but wouldn't come in. He was an important man, and refused to be seen with me for fear of scandal. He made me put down a fake name and undergo the procedure. Afterwards he picked me up, and later that night he came into my room and mocked my religion, telling me how un-Catholic my actions were. I took this criticism seriously and believed I was going to hell. For years afterwards, I had nightmares of my unborn child calling my name.

The years passed in misery, and when the date of my appointment with immigration drew near, my husband told me he would not attend the meeting with me unless I performed in bed with him and another girl. Without him at that meeting, I wasn't going to get my green card. He had me trapped, but even when he brought another woman home, I still refused. I was seized with rage—at my husband, at the situation, at my parents for giving birth to me in such misery, and at God who had subjected me to a life of slavery, rape, violence, and horror. I broke everything in my room, perfume, lamps, bowls, everything. Finally, I called my sister and told her not to look for me when I disappeared. I had decided to kill myself.

There is a lake off Route 30 going toward Marlboro, Massachusetts, and I had often contemplated driving my car at high speed through the barrier into the water, to end everything once and for all. Often I would go in the early morning, before many cars were driving past. I would park, and circle around the steaming lake, looking for a good spot to throw myself off, checking for rocks and even trying to see which area was the deepest. This time, still talking to my sister, I got in my car and began driving there, with the intent to die that afternoon.

My sister pleaded with me, and put my twelve-year-old nephew on the phone, who was crying and trying to get me to stop. My sister had told him what I was going to do, and it broke my heart to hear him pleading with me for my life. "Please, Auntie, do not do this thing," he cried, his rich accent marred by sobs. Surely I couldn't kill myself while I talked to him. So I began to slow down, letting the cars along the freeway pass me, ignoring their honking, which I barely even heard. Soon I pulled over on the shoulder and stopped. By then my sister was back on the phone, telling me to call my lawyer.

My sister eventually convinced me, and I called him. His secretary picked up the phone, and in my panicked state I told her everything, how I was on my way to kill myself, how I was trapped in this marriage. She comforted me and kept me on the phone. Meanwhile, she paged the lawyer, who soon called me, too. He told me about a law that exists, whereby women who are bound to an abusive husband for reasons of citizenship are allowed to terminate the marriage and still obtain a green card, provided proof of mistreatment and legal grounds for the granting of citizenship can be shown in court.

This law was designed for people like me, because people like my husband exist, who take advantage of women in my situation, too desperate to resist. The problem is that few people know about these laws. My lawyer convinced me there was a way out, without giving in anymore to my husband's demands. In doing so, he talked me out of suicide. I returned home, packed a bag, and went to stay with my sister. The next day we obtained a restraining order against my husband, and later the divorce was finalized. I entered a shelter for battered women who have to stay hidden from their husbands. I disappeared from the world for about a year. After hiding, I returned to my town, rented a house, and have been, again, adjusting to living on my own. I work full-time as a nurse, and keeping up with the bills keeps me busy. Still, I'm happy, and I'm free.

I never saw my husband again after that night, and ever since, God has been working in me to make me love myself again. I began therapy as soon as I entered the shelter, and it took a good six months, maybe longer, to realize that what I had been subjected to was not my fault. Today, I am confident and convinced of my own worth. But the shadows of doubt still haunt me.

I have become an active lobbyist fighting human trafficking in America, and continue to work closely with local government representatives. One reason for writing my story is to call attention to the plight of women like myself who are victimized by trafficking networks. There exist people who seek to use others for their own profit. These traffickers thrive on the ignorance of others, and the best way to combat them is to make potential victims aware that such predators exist. Human trafficking and slavery are just two examples of the dangers young, poor women face.

Behind closed doors there is often someone suffering. These people often cannot or will not help themselves. The public must seek out these places and must work to change systems that prey on young women and immigrants. Immigrant women do not need to stay in abusive marriages to gain citizenship, but most of them don't know that. The duty to open their eyes falls on us.

Slattery's ability to transcend a dizzying array of obstacles throughout her life is nothing short of remarkable. Once degraded as worthless, she is now an influential force driving the contemporary abolitionist movement, speaking out about her experience in order to raise awareness. In 2006, Slattery was welcomed by her former high school in Norwalk, Connecticut, where she recounted her years of enslavement while a student at the school. There, Slattery challenged the sizable Haitian community of Norwalk to deconstruct the abusive restavec *system and work for the freedom of child slaves.*

Chapter Two

BEYOND ABEEDA

SURVIVING TEN YEARS
OF SLAVERY IN SUDAN

Abuk Bak

Sudan, the largest country in Africa, straddles the fault-line of North Africa's dominant Arab identity and the black African identity of the southern part of the continent. The name "Sudan" is Arabic for "land of the blacks," and race relations in the country are strained and complicated, charged in part by a centuries-old history of Arab slave raids on African villages. The fact that many southerners are Christian adds a religious dynamic to the country's internal conflicts.

In the early 1980s, the Arab-dominated government in Sudan imposed Islamic law on the entire country. Much of the

African south rose up in rebellion, refusing to submit to sharia *rules. The ruling regime's response was brutal, and in the following two decades over two million people were killed and four million made refugees, primarily in the south. One of the government's key tactics was the revival of slave raids against African villages in the South, a practice that had largely been stopped during British colonial rule in the early twentieth century. Militias armed by the Sudanese government destroyed entire villages and individual militiamen were allowed to take women and children as plunder. Thousands upon thousands of African civilians caught up in the militia raids suddenly found themselves held as slaves, to be kept by militiamen or sold off.*

In 1987, Abuk Bak, then a twelve-year-old girl, was captured in one of these slave raids. In her testimony below, she recounts in detail both the terrifying raid and the subsequent decade she spent in slavery. Hers is one of the few accounts of child slavery in this collection, although millions of children are caught up in modern-day slavery around the world. Bak today is free, yet in Sudan alone thousands of women and children remain in bondage.

Today, the Sudan genocide—particularly the flare-up in Darfur—is a prominent international issue. But in 1987, the world ignored the raid on Bak's village. No international media reported on it, no United Nations investigation was launched, and no demonstrations were held in protest (read more about this in the epilogue). Bak was abducted and the international community stayed silent and largely oblivious. Yet, since regaining her freedom, Bak has been determined to break the silence: protesting outside the UN, speaking on college campuses, and even confronting Sudanese diplomats. Though she has been profiled in Ladies Home Journal *and on* Oxygen TV, *this chapter marks the first complete retelling of her ordeal. Bak sat down for exten-*

sive interviews with writer Rebecca Hansen, revealing painful details she had never discussed before.

"My name is Abuk Bak." These are the words I said to Khiddir Ahmed, the Sudanese ambassador to the United States, when he came to Tufts University for a conference on Sudan in March 2004. I had made my way through a crowd of people to reach him and knew I only had a minute to get his attention. "As a child I was enslaved for ten years in Sudan," I told him, and handed him a letter I had written asking for reparations from the Sudanese government.

"You are a liar," he said, looking straight into my eyes, "There is no slavery in Sudan." Then he turned his back on me and walked out of the room. He took my letter with him, but I'm sure he never read it.

I was saddened by his reaction, but not surprised. And, I told myself, the day had not been a waste. I told my story and the story of my village, Achuru, to a group of people who had come to protest the policies of the Sudanese government and, unlike Khiddir Ahmed, none of them denied the truth of my story, or the existence of slavery in Sudan.

My hope, the reason why I speak out whenever I can, is that those people will do more than just listen, that they will raise their voices along with me. My hope is that, together, we will have the power to make people like Khiddir Ahmed turn and face the truth. That is why I tell my story.

There was nothing unusual about seeing Northern Arab men in Achuru; their loose white robes and layered turbans were a familiar sight to us. We lived far from Sudan's capital, Khartoum, two or three weeks on foot if I remember right.

So they came to trade tea, sugar, and clothes, things we couldn't make ourselves. I knew nothing about the raids that some of these same men were conducting all over Southern Sudan. If I had, I might have been more frightened of the rifles they carried with them.

One day, my grandfather, the head of my community, heard the news about a village very close to ours being raided. He told me that a militia had come from the North and killed all the men, burned their houses to the ground, and taken the women, children, and animals with them to the North. To protect us, he took everyone into the jungle to hide, including all of our animals, the cows and goats. I didn't feel any safer out there. I worried that the militiamen could find us in the jungle. I also knew lions lived there too, a danger that seemed more real to me than the idea of my village being burned to the ground.

I had never actually seen a lion, but heard stories from adults who went to the jungle to gather wood. They would tell the children they had heard a lion's roar or seen a tiger because they had gone too far into the jungle. "Don't go too far from the village!" my mother or another grown-up would tell us. "The lions will eat you up!" At the time I believed their stories, being all of twelve years old, though now I think that some of them were made up to scare us into staying close to home, and it worked. Leaving Achuru for the jungle was frightening, but it was what we had to do.

My entire village stayed in the jungle for about a month. Each morning, the men would go back to the village and make sure that no one had been there. We, the women and children, had to be quiet as mice all day and all night. I tried not to make any sounds, and if a baby coughed or cried I did my best to comfort and quiet it. These were long, hard days, and after so much time without any sign of problems in the village, my grandfather brought us back home.

The next day the militiamen came.

The first morning after we returned to my village I felt nervous, but also happy to be back in my home and able to play and laugh and run freely again. I was playing outside of my house with my cousin, my brother, and my sister when I heard the first gunshot and the air filled with sounds of horse hooves pounding on the dirt.

"It's a gun!" my cousin shouted, recognizing the sound from when the men in the village went out to hunt giraffe or elephants. The militiamen, wrapped in their white robes and turbans, were shooting every man who crossed their path and setting fire to our houses, which, with their thatched, grass roofs, went up in flames instantly.

"Run! Run!" everyone screamed at me, but I didn't know which way to go; the men on horseback seemed to be coming from all sides. The four of us that had been playing scattered in a panic. I ran as fast as I could, looking in every direction for my mother and father.

Achuru lies between two streams and you have to cross one of them in order to reach the jungle, so everyone was heading toward the crossing point. I followed the crowd, surrounded by my friends and family, all running and screaming, with the pounding of horse hooves and gunshots coming from close behind. At some point I felt a hand grab mine and looked up to see my aunt, carrying her baby against her chest as she tried to pull me along even faster.

My grandmother and grandfather ran up next to us, but soon one of the Arab militiamen on horseback spotted my grandfather among the women and children. He fired his gun and my grandfather was shot dead before my eyes.

When I turned to go back to him, I felt a rope fall and tighten around my waist. I struggled to free myself but the rope was too strong, and I watched as my aunt was lassoed by the same man.

"Abeeda!" the militiaman screamed at me over and over, along with a stream of Arabic words that I couldn't understand. The word meant nothing to me at the time, though it would soon become part of my daily life. Ten years would pass before I learned its meaning: black slave.

The man who had captured me and my aunt did not slow his horse down for us, and so we ran behind, trying to keep up and stay on our feet as the ropes pulled us along by our waists. While I ran I looked back and saw that the stream had worked like a trap for my entire village, forcing those who had made it there alive to slow down as they tried to cross. Stopped along the edge of the stream, most people could not escape the guns and ropes of the men on horseback.

When the raid was finished, my aunt and I were taken from the village together with many other women and children from Achuru. We walked all day with no food or water. Shouts of *Abeeda!* rang in our ears as we tried to keep up with the fast pace of the horses. All I could think of was my family. Where were my mother and father? Had they survived? Were my brothers and sisters somewhere in this group? My cousins? The image of my grandfather falling to the ground kept flashing in front of my eyes.

That night we arrived at the market in a town called Daien. The militiamen herded us all into a large pen surrounded by a grass thatch fence, which reminded me of the roofs of our homes in Achuru that had been set aflame by the same men earlier in the day. I stayed close to my aunt, wondering where my mother and father were, my brothers and sisters, wondering if I would see them or my village ever again.

I passed the night without sleeping. In the morning, more Arab men came and spoke with the militiamen who had raided my village, though I couldn't understand what they were saying. It seemed as though they were old friends. Each time the men came back the word spread like fire through the crowd, and everyone sat down, trying to stay low and out of sight. We quickly learned to stay quiet and try to stay hidden, although there was nowhere for us to hide.

The turbaned men observed us and pointed at different people, choosing which person they wanted to buy, the same way they chose their goats and cows from the pens around us. They didn't bother to look us over to see if we were healthy or strong; if we got sick or died they could just buy someone else to do their work.

I watched them as they yelled and pointed until finally they settled on a deal. Then one of the Arabs from the raid would charge in between us and drag one of us out to her new master. I heard the word again, *Abeeda, Abeeda.* They also watched us to make sure we didn't make any trouble or try to escape. If anyone did, they would be beaten or killed. While all this went on I sat quietly, making myself as small as I could against the body of my aunt. I didn't know where these men were taking people, but it was nowhere I wanted to go, and no one came back.

When it came my turn to be picked out of the crowd, I panicked. I screamed and cried and tried to hang on to my aunt and she clung to me, but we could not match the strength of the grown men or the guns that they pointed at us. The guards brought me to a man who had purchased me for an unknown price.

He would be my master for the next ten years.

Just looking at him scared me to death. He had a thick salt and pepper beard that covered most of his face and, though I couldn't see his mouth to tell if he was smiling, the hard look in his eyes made me sure that he was not. He seemed about forty years old, and with his tall, broad body he towered over me.

After the long walk the day before and a sleepless night with no food or water, the journey to this man's house was exhausting. He lived several miles from the market, and though I had no rope around my waist this time, he used a whip to keep me moving. Because I was a child and wore only the customary skirt of my village, there was nothing to stand between the skin of my back and the stinging leather rope. Whenever I slowed down my new master would yell, "Abeeda!" and snap the whip hard against my back to keep me moving. He also whipped me if I looked around to see who and what we were passing by. I had to keep my eyes on the ground in front of me, so I don't know if I passed any other Dinka slaves that day. I imagine that my new owner wouldn't have wanted me to see them if I did. We might have spoken to each other or tried to help each other or run away.

When we arrived at the house, I realized how far I had come from Achuru. Everything about this place was different from home. Where the land in my village had been green, rich with plants and fruit trees, this land was desert, brown and bare. It was covered in sand with a few blades of grass here and there, but nothing like the lush land of Southern Sudan. The house looked so strange to me compared to the round, raised houses of stucco and thatch I had grown up in. It was more like a very large tent, made from cow leather—maybe from cows stolen from villages like my own, I thought.

When the man brought me to the house to show the family his new purchase, I saw that he had two children, a boy and a girl, who looked only a few years younger than me, maybe nine or ten. I hoped that maybe they would be my friends here in this new place, someone to play with. But when I heard their tiny voices just like their father's— *Abeeda! Abeeda!*—I felt even more alone.

I realized from listening to the man and his wife talk to each other that his name was Ahmed Adam and hers was Aisha, though they never bothered to learn mine. To them I was just *abeeda.*

Aisha seemed several years younger than Ahmed Adam, though her face was hidden. She took me around the house and showed me with gestures what my responsibilities would be. She showed me how to wash the clothes and the dishes, how to sweep the floor and clean the house, where the needles and thread were for sewing. Each time, she put the soap, the broom, or the needle in my hands after the lesson and watched to make sure that I had learned what to do.

That night they fed me leftover scraps from their dinner, pieces of uneaten fat from their meat or the hot water they had used for boiling vegetables. It was a terrible meal, one that I would often reject in the years to come, but it didn't matter to me that night. No one had given me anything to eat or drink since being taken from my village and, that first evening, I ate everything they gave me.

I ate my meager dinner on the patch of dirt a few yards from the house where Ahmed Adam had shown me I would be sleeping. There was no blanket, no roof or even a tent, just a space in the dirt that would be mine. In spite of my exhaustion, I still couldn't sleep that first night. I had gone to bed hungry, as I would almost every night as a slave, and my mind was as full of fear and questions as it had been since the raid, just two days before.

So much had changed so fast. I still thought constantly about my family and wondered what would happen to me. Would I be taken somewhere else? Would I be killed in the morning? I thought I would never stop crying. I considered trying to escape, but I had no idea where I was or where I could go. It was dark, and when I imagined running away, I remembered my mother's warnings about tigers and lions. I feared that if I got caught I would be killed. I was only twelve, scared and alone. I could not see any way out.

The next morning, Ahmed Adam woke me up before sunrise to show me the work that I had to do for him in addition to taking care of the house. Like his wife, he used hand motions and showed me how to take his goats out and find good grazing and watering places, a difficult task in such dry land. He spoke as he made these motions, though I couldn't understand anything he said. At first I tried to speak back to him and ask questions in Dinka, but whenever I did he got angry and beat me—with his fist, a stick, or a whip, whatever was around. I learned quickly that staying silent would make my life easier.

Starting from that first day Ahmed Adam tried to teach me the Arabic I would need to pray with him and his family, but I didn't understand and didn't want to. He made me wash my hands and face and kneel down with them, but because I didn't know the meaning behind their words or their actions I refused and pulled away. He beat me before letting me go, but that seemed better than taking part in things that I didn't understand. For several days he tried to make me pray with the family, but each time I pulled away and each time he beat me, until he finally gave up.

On my second day there Ahmed Adam sent me out alone with the goats. It didn't matter to him that I was only twelve years old, that I had no idea where I was, or that I had never done this kind of work before. It would now be my job to take care of about twenty animals and to see that every one of them returned home. I didn't think of this until the first time I came back with one animal missing. When Ahmed Adam counted and realized that I had lost a goat, he beat me severely with a stick and then sent me out into the night to search for the missing goat.

I walked out into the dark, my skin stinging from the blows. I didn't want to be beaten again, but I was even more frightened of the lions and wild animals, so I didn't go far. When I was just out of sight of the house I found a place to hide and waited. When I thought enough time had passed for a good search, I came back to Ahmed Adam. He saw that I had come back empty-handed and beat me again before letting me go to my place to sleep. There was nothing I could do to stop him.

From then on I worked in constant fear: fear that a lion could come out of the grass and attack an animal or me, and fear of the beating that I would get whenever one of the goats wandered off without my realizing, which they often did. This fear only got worse when Ahmed Adam put me in charge of his cattle as well as the goats. I was no match for a group of thirty to forty animals of that size with such sharp hooves and horns. I often came back to the house with bruises and cuts from where they had kicked me.

With something like sixty animals to keep track of, I never knew if I had lost one until I got home and Ahmed Adam counted. That moment of the day was always one of the worst for me, waiting to see if I would get a beating, not knowing whether I would have to go back out into the darkness or if I would be allowed to go to my patch of dirt and wait for my leftovers. No matter how many times I got a beating, I never once searched for the missing animals, knowing that it would be crazy for me to wander around in the night by myself. But I had to at least pretend. Otherwise, I feared Ahmed Adam might get even angrier and kill me.

Doing the housework for Aisha was sometimes just as scary as working with the animals. Although it wasn't physically as hard as running after the goats and trying to keep the cattle together, I was so exhausted from tending the animals that I often made mistakes with the housework. Doing the dishes is an easy job after you've had a nice meal and you're comfortable in your own home, but for me it was a frightening challenge. My arms ached and, sometimes, a wet soapy dish would slip from my fingers and break on the floor. This always meant a beating from Ahmed Adam or his wife. Though Aisha had seemed quiet at first, she became much more demanding and aggressive with me when Ahmed Adam wasn't around.

The children, too, would beat me whenever they felt like it or when they were bored. Sometimes their father would call me over and the children would kick and push me, yelling *Abeeda!* as they had learned to do from their father. When they got tired of beating me they would run away

50

laughing, and Ahmed Adam would send me back to whatever work had been interrupted. *Abeeda.* I still did not understand what that word meant, but I knew it was only meant for me.

On many days, especially in the beginning, I felt too sad to care about eating, or whether or not the scraps that I got at the end of the day were any good. But, on other days, my body needed much more than the small amount of food they gave me. I tried to look for fruit while out with the animals, but this land was so different from my village, where I could easily find a ripe orange or mango. Out here there was nothing.

Sometimes while working in the house, I would sneak food, a small piece of beef or bread, if I thought no one could see me. I felt frightened, but I had grown used to being scared most of the time and was too hungry to care. The first day that Ahmed Adam caught me, he wrapped his hands tightly around my neck, choking me and making me spit the food back out, screaming at me in words I couldn't understand. But fear of a beating didn't stop me from sneaking food again—most of the time my hunger was stronger than my fear.

The loneliness of my life with Ahmed Adam and his family was overwhelming. I would go days, even weeks at a time without speaking to anyone. It took me years to understand any part of the few words they said to me. Even the word *abeeda* was still a mystery to me with no one there to explain its meaning. After I refused to learn to pray with the Koran, Ahmed Adam stopped trying to teach me anything, and my days were filled with silence.

When I was out with the animals, I would sing to myself the Dinka songs that I learned in my childhood. At night, sometimes I would sit in the patch of dirt and play games silently by myself. I would dream that I was back in Achuru, speaking in Dinka with my friends and family. I missed the time we used to spend together playing games, telling stories, and laughing. In the end, those memories only made me feel worse.

After several years of living with Ahmed Adam and his family, I had grown used to my daily routine of working with the animals and doing chores in the house, as well as the frequent beatings. While I still thought every day of my family and wondered if I would see them again, I never thought seriously about trying to escape.

In certain parts of the North, I now know, many slaves lived close to one another and saw other Dinka people in their daily work and travels, but I was not so lucky. In all my wanderings to find good grass and water for the animals, I never saw another person. After so many long years I still had no idea where I was, or where to go if I left, and I was too scared to try. But that would soon change.

Because I had grown older and looked more like a woman than a child, Ahmed Adam began to look at me in a different way. He started coming out to where I slept at night, though not very often at first. It was strange for me to see him without the white head cover of his turban. Though he removed it every day to pray, I wasn't always there. At night I could look closely at his balding head and the dark spot on the middle of his forehead from where he had pressed it to the ground so many times.

When he first came to me at night, all I had to do was make a little noise and he would run back to the house. He was so afraid that his wife would find out what he was trying to do that he quickly went back inside and left me alone.

But, as time went on, he appeared more often and became more demanding and less afraid. Now even the night became a time of fear, as I never knew when I would awake to find him beside me.

This pattern continued for a few years until, one night, Ahmed Adam went too far. He came out and threw himself on top of me before I could yell and scare him away. He whispered sharply in my ear that I should be quiet and covered my mouth with his sweaty hand so I couldn't scream. He pushed me down but I pushed back at him with my arms and feet. He was taller than me, and bigger, but my fear and anger made me just as strong.

As we struggled, Ahmed Adam grabbed the knife that he carried in his sleeve and stabbed me in my right thigh. The pain was so strong that he could not stop my screams, and he ran back into the house, afraid that his wife would hear.

Ahmed Adam had opened a wound in my thigh that was four or five inches long and almost as wide. I knew right away that I would not stay to see another morning there, but my leg was bleeding badly. I ripped a piece of cloth from my skirt and tied it around my thigh to try to stop the bleeding, and thought about how to escape. I lay awake all night, knowing that if I ran away I could be found and severely beaten or killed, but I had to take a chance.

Before dawn, I left the yard. I found my way to a road, trying to ignore the sharp pain in my leg, and walked until I came to a truck that was stopped off to the side. It was full of goats and smelled terrible, but I managed to sneak on and crawled to the back behind all of the animals where no one would see me. I had no idea where the truck was going, or what would happen to me when I got there. Wherever we stopped, I knew I could be caught and sold to a new master or brought back to Ahmed Adam, either of which would mean more beatings and more labor. I promised myself that I would not go back to that life.

When the truck finally stopped I crouched as low as I could and sneaked out the back to find myself in a busy market, which I would later learn was in a town called Babanusa. I was surrounded by Northern Arab men doing business of one kind or another, and I could barely breathe for fear. What if someone saw me? I certainly did not blend in with the crowd of men in white robes and turbans. But, as I began to make my way through the people, I saw some Southern Sudanese faces mixed in with the Northern Arab ones. I could tell them apart by their darker skin and the way they were dressed, in shirts and pants. I picked a man out of the crowd who I knew must be from Southern Sudan, though I had no idea whether he was Dinka or from some other tribe. Not knowing whether he would understand, I spoke.

"Ci yi bak," I said to him, waving my hand as I used the Dinka word for "hello" for the first time in ten years. Before he had a chance to answer I felt the words rushing out. "I've been enslaved by an Arab man since my village was raided ten years ago and I escaped last night. I'm running away and I don't know where to go, I need help."

"What's your name?" he asked me in Dinka.

"Abuk Bak Macam," I answered.

His response seemed incredible. "I know your grandfather," he said, recognizing the last name that had been passed down to me by my grandfather. He told me that his name was Majak and that he had been to Achuru as a child; he came from a village only one day's walk away. "I remember when your village was raided," he said.

I felt both excited to have found someone connected to my family and saddened at the memory of my grandfather's murder. Thinking of it reminded me of the danger of my situation, something that Majak thought of as well. He said that the market was not a safe place for me and that he would help me get out. He bought me a train ticket to Khartoum and brought me to stay with his family. They lived in the tent camps set up by the United Nations outside of Khartoum, where tens of thousands of Southern Sudanese refugees had come to escape the militia raids.

Majak and his family took me in, bought me clothes, and helped me look for my mother and father. They let me stay with them and keep looking for my family—every day hundreds of Southern Sudanese people arrived in the refugee camps. Majak had four children, so we were crowded in the small tent house, but I didn't mind. I was happy to be away from Ahmed Adam and back with my own people, and it felt amazing to speak my own language again.

Majak knew some Arabic after living in Khartoum for a few years. When I realized this, I asked him, "Do you know what *abeeda* means?"

"It means black slave," he said.

When I heard this, I felt sad and angry to think that such a word had been forced upon me for so many years, but I knew it would do me no good to think about the past. Instead, I looked to the future. I was not *abeeda* any more, and I never would be again.

Every day I went out to look for my family. This wasn't easy, because the stab wound in my leg was not healed and still very painful. I washed it with saltwater to keep it clean and Majak's wife bought me medicine to help with the pain, but it was difficult to walk. Still, I made my way around the camp and asked everyone if they knew my father and mother. I met many people from my village, but no one had heard anything about my family.

After a few days, I realized that it was no safer to be in the tent camps than it had been in my village. The Northern Arab police patrolled the camps constantly and used any excuse to beat people or take them away. Although people from the United Nations came around to give us water and other supplies, they did not provide us with any protection. We had to look out for ourselves and we lived in fear of the police.

Some of the people in the camp drank alcohol, but since it goes against Muslim law, getting caught meant a terrible beating. Police would come to the camps looking for young boys to force into the same militias that had killed their families. Any boy who had reached the age of fifteen or sixteen was in danger of being taken by the military whenever he stepped outside his tent. Majak also told me that the police sometimes came looking for escaped slaves, and if someone recognized me, I could get taken back to Ahmed Adam or be beaten or killed. When I was not looking for my family, I stayed inside the tent to avoid any trouble or contact with the police.

I stayed with Majak and his family for five months, searching for my family every day but never hearing any news of them. Majak finally suggested that I go to Catholic Choice, a group in Khartoum that helps slavery survivors get a Sudanese passport so that they can travel to Egypt. I knew I could not live with Majak forever. I wanted to start my own life, but it was not an easy process. In general, the government in Sudan does not like the idea of an unmarried woman traveling and making plans on her own, so each time I brought the necessary forms and papers to the embassy, they gave me more to fill out.

Finally, Majak told me that his brother, Atak, lived in Cairo, and that he and I could get married. This would make it much easier for me to get the necessary permits to travel. I agreed because I could see by then that Majak was a good person, and the fact that he had known my grandfather and my parents made me feel even more connected to him. I imagined that, if my parents had been there to arrange the marriage as was the custom in my village, they would have approved of a match with Atak.

As soon as Majak told the consul that I was his brother's wife, although we were technically not married yet, I was granted a passport and allowed to travel. Still, I had to buy a two-way ticket in order to make the government think that I would be coming back, which of course I wasn't.

When the time came to leave I had mixed feelings. I knew that by going to Cairo and marrying Atak I would finally begin my own life, but part of me didn't want to leave my country, or abandon the possibility of finding my family. Each day brought hope of finding my mother or father among the new refugee arrivals.

I also had mixed feelings about marrying Atak, not because I doubted that he was a good person, but because I couldn't have a wedding in my village with my family there to see. As a child in Achuru my grandmother and grandfather had told me stories of what my wedding day would be like, and I had imagined that important day many times.

In my village, when a girl turns eighteen, her family talks with other families and decides on a man who will make a good match, usually someone from a family that they have known for a long time. The two families agree on a dowry to be paid for the bride, which is usually a number of cattle (this was how we measured wealth in my village). For me, the dowry would have been high, around 200 cattle, because I was the oldest girl in my family and would have been the first to marry. At our weddings we ate well, laughed a lot, made music, and danced together. Everyone brought gifts for the bride and groom. It's also the day that the bride becomes a woman. In my village, all of the children wear small cloths around their waist, but on the day of a girl's wedding, she wears a full, long dress to show that she is not a child anymore.

In Cairo, I wouldn't have many of these things. But I imagined that my family would approve of the match that I had made, since Majak had known my grandfather and there was a connection between our two families.

The trip to meet Atak in Cairo lasted three weeks. I traveled by train, then by bus, then by boat for four days to cross the Nile, then by bus again to Cairo. Through all that traveling I wondered about my future husband. I had never even seen a picture of Atak, who, like me, had fled Sudan in fear of the government. Rather than be forced by the Arab militias to turn a gun on his own people, as many of the young boys in the camps had been, Atak and others like him fled to Cairo. He had been living there for several years already when I went to meet him. I felt so nervous wondering what he would look and sound like, what kind of personality he would have.

When I arrived in Cairo, there was a crowd of people waiting for the bus. I looked around at all the faces but had no idea which one belonged to Atak.

"Are you Abuk?" I heard someone ask and looked to see a face that looked like Majak's smiling back at me. I knew it must be him. He took my bag and brought me home to his apartment. It felt strange to be there, in the home of a complete stranger who would soon become my husband.

Atak and I got married in a church in Cairo. Catholic Choice gave me a white dress to wear and Atak bought a blue grey suit for himself. We invited about 50 Southern Sudanese who were friends and neighbors of Atak and we had good food and laughed and danced. Part of me felt very happy, but part of me felt sad that my family was not there to see me get married. My mind returned again and again to my mother and father, to my grandfather and my village, to the wedding I had always imagined. I tried to think about the happy things, though, and how lucky I was to have escaped after ten years of slavery.

Not long after our wedding, Atak and I received refugee status from the United Nations and moved to the United States. With Majak's help, I finally found my mother, sister, and brother, and now we live together in Massachusetts. My husband and I work hard. We have a nice home and three beautiful children who will have a good life here.

But I remember Sudan. Every day I think about the women and children who are still enslaved there, about my grandfather and the men who are still being killed, about Southern Sudanese boys forced to fight against their own people. I think about my father, who remained in Southern Sudan after the raid and is still trying to get refugee status so that he can reunite with us in the United States.

The terrible things that happened to me, my family, and my village are still happening in Sudan today, and though I am far away from it all, I know my voice has power. Many people have no idea what is happening in Sudan, or even where it is, but I am working to change that. Although people like Ambassador Ahmed might want to ignore me and my story, there are many others who will listen, and I will continue to raise my voice. I will speak out about what is happening to the people in my country until the raids and the violence and the slavery have stopped. I don't know if this will happen in my lifetime, but I still dream of taking my children back to meet my father, who has never seen them. I dream of returning to my village one day. And I dream that, maybe, when enough people raise their voices with me, I and my country will find peace.

Despite raising three children and working long hours, Bak speaks regularly at schools, congregations, and rallies about her experience. She reminds audiences that thousands of women and children are still held in slavery in Sudan, and she calls on Americans to help set them free. She is still awaiting a response from the Sudanese ambassador.

Chapter Three

MY LIFE AS A SLAVE IN AMERICA

Jill Leighton

In 1978, FBI agents in Miami discovered Rose Iftony, a young girl from Sierra Leone, kept as a domestic slave inside the house of a Pakistani couple. At the time, one agent described Iftony's bondage as "the first classic case of slavery [in the United States] this century that the FBI knows of."

It would not be the last. Instead, the years that followed have seen a steady rise in cases of slavery in the United States. Instances of contemporary American slavery typically involve foreigners trafficked into the United States (like Rose Iftony). But sometimes those trapped in bondage are native-born Americans.

Just a few years after Rose Iftony was rescued in Miami, Jill Leighton found herself lured into slavery. In the no-holds-barred excerpt that follows, Leighton recounts how she became trapped as a sex slave. What begins as a seemingly innocent encounter quickly escalates into ruthless abuse. Readers are forewarned that Leighton's narrative is an explicit chronicle of her ordeal. It is also a powerful reminder that cases of slavery are occurring today in communities across the United States.

PROLOGUE

In 1981, I became a statistic: I became a runaway teen, escaping sexual and physical abuse. When I ran away, I no longer had a place to live with my parents nor did I have a living relative who would take me in. Filled with a sense of bravado, invincibility, and bravery, I left, figuring that my life couldn't be in any more jeopardy than it already was at what I'd called home. In leaving I hoped there would be no more broken bones, no more sexual abuse, no more rationalizations of molestation and cruelty. When I left that day, I had no more than a change of clothes and less than one hundred dollars. No longer did my name, childhood identity, school, or grades matter. All became irrelevant in the world I was about to enter.

As a runaway at age fourteen, your old concerns quickly disappear and are replaced by new, life-threatening ones. There were no familiar faces and no one who wanted to talk to a teenage girl who was homeless; even my name became irrelevant. Instead, my concerns were more pragmatic: finding food, shelter, and water, and passing time without the money to financially support these needs. I'd resorted to sleeping in cemeteries and stealing food out of dumpsters and from convenience stores in order to eat. Getting drinking water and a chance to wash my face became quests of endurance. I had to hide from security guards, store and restaurant employees, and others who didn't want a homeless girl "loitering." I was viewed as something less than human. Still, it was safer than going home.

JULY 3, 1981—DAY 1

The manipulation began within minutes of meeting him. His eyes were penetrating. His dark, curly, shoulder-length hair and neatly trimmed beard gave him an appearance strikingly similar to Lindsay Buckingham of Fleetwood Mac. It was like meeting Lindsay, the guy I had such a huge crush on. His name was Bruce. He began by being sweet. I felt like he could read my mind. Within a few minutes I had told him my entire life's story.

In a few minutes Bruce had done what the high school guidance counselor and my parish priest hadn't done. He listened to me pour out my heart, telling him about the molestation I'd faced at home. He listened to me tell him about the physical, emotional, and sexual abuse. Unlike the high school guidance counselor, who silenced me with the admonition that my "story" could cause a scandal and provoke my father—a member of the local school board—to retaliate by voting against school funding issues, Bruce expressed outrage at the guidance counselor's callous disregard of my pain. Unlike the parish priest the guidance counselor referred me to, Bruce never told me to keep my pain between myself and the Almighty. "Tell it to the Almighty, Jill" was the parish priest's only advice. The same priest that gave Communion to my family and me every week.

Bruce soaked up my pain, my fear, my anger like a sponge, repeating it back to me with the empathic skills of a counselor. No one had ever treated me as if they cared at the level he did. No one had ever told me all the things he told me in the two hours that we talked. He praised my maturity, my beauty, my intelligence, my professionalism, my courage in the face of hardship.

After two hours of flattery and attention, Bruce had a proposal: a job as an actress, a place to stay with him, food, shelter, and affection. All I had to do was go with him to his office and audition for the job. He reassured me that his position as owner of the entertainment agency virtually guaranteed I would be given a position. Of course I would have to pay rent and expenses out of my earnings, but I could enter school locally, and work on nights, weekends and vacations.

I expressed one concern. I asked him if the position was prostitution. In a second everything changed. The charming gentleman became harsh and cold with the abrupt announcement that I had misled him. I was not professional or mature. Just an immature spoiled brat who just "insulted the best thing that had ever happened to me."

I was horrified and couldn't believe my stupidity. I ran up to him and begged his forgiveness for my insult with a desperate promise to never again insult him with stupid questions or attacks on his character of the nature I had just committed. Of course I knew this wasn't prostitution. What kind of man did I think he was? It was all my fault and I tearfully promised nothing of the sort would ever happen again. With a kiss on the cheek all was forgiven and we walked out to his car.

I got into his car and he handed me a pair of blinding sunglasses to wear. I told him I was okay, but he was insistent; operating the most successful entertainment agency in the Tri-States region left him vulnerable to corporate spies from other agencies. They couldn't know the location of his office because they would then be able to burglarize his agency and steal his client list. Therefore, I would have to be blindfolded for the drive in the event that either of us felt the job wasn't a good fit.

While being blindfolded scared me, I quickly agreed. My transgression of just a few minutes ago was fresh in my mind, and I could not offend him again. Of course I was safe with him. Even if I was blindfolded. I was terrified of displaying any emotion that wasn't mature and professional. Therefore, I did what he told me to do and let him blindfold me, with a smile and faux bravado to make it clear that I could handle this with maturity.

The alleged ride to his downtown office didn't sound right as we traveled on a warm summer day. The sounds I could hear outside the car were suburban. Bruce must have concluded that I was afraid despite my attempt to demonstrate bravery. He became the sweet, kind man that he had been in the mall for the duration of our trip. He talked with me about how scared he realized I must be, bolstering my spirits with the statement that I was handling the stress as well as he had ever seen. We talked about music that I liked. He shared similar taste and knew all of my favorites. Stevie Nicks, Pat Benatar, Juice Newton.

Still, while we shared this discussion my instincts continued to tell me something was wrong. There were many starts and stops in traffic, with continued requests from Bruce to sit lower in the bucket seat of his car. Finally we stopped. The thought of taking off the blindfold or trying to get out of the car was in the back of my mind. But without any viable alternative and fearing the potential of angering Bruce, I made no effort to escape.

Bruce told me we were going into the parking garage of his office building but the sounds betrayed his statement. It sounded like a garage door going up, then closing. Still, I remained quiet while Bruce got out of the car and opened my door. Guiding me through a doorway and down a wooden set of stairs, he kept describing his lower-level audition and talent screening room. It felt all wrong. The sounds didn't add up. The smell was the musty, moldy smell of a basement that had unresolved water issues.

Throughout the drive I had remained stoic in my emotions. Now fear had overtaken my sense of bravado and willingness to please. The tears that began to flow in the garage were seeping below my blindfold. The thought of him taking the blindfold off scared me because I was crying and didn't want him to notice.

It was too late. Bruce was angry again, demanding to know why I was crying. Once again I had given offense. Why was I crying? Hadn't he been completely respectful to me? Did he ever once try to touch me? What was wrong with me that I was so insistent on insulting someone who just wanted to help? The interrogation only made the crying worse and I could feel the blindfold starting to shift from the tears. Bruce angrily denounced my behavior as childish, unprofessional, and disrespectful of all the kindness I had been shown.

My desperation fueled statements of self-deprecation, but my apologies for my acts of immaturity and disrespect were going nowhere. I had failed and was in danger of losing the opportunity. Fortunately for me, Bruce said there was another option: a dance audition and photo session. It would require a dance on stage with just my underwear to prove my lack of fear. Prove my trust. Prove my professionalism.

I did what he said and prayed that he didn't notice that I was shaking. Bruce noticed and was angry about it. Grabbing my hands really hard he wrapped something around both wrists and told me to hold still. Before I had a chance to think about what was going to happen next, something went totally wrong. My feet weren't touching the floor anymore. My shoulders suddenly exploded in pain and it became almost impossible to breath.

I didn't initially understand what had happened. I was instantly disoriented by pain in my shoulders and an inability to get my feet on the ground. I could hardly breathe. It was as if there was too much weight on my chest. But that wasn't it. Was I upside down? I kept seeing flashes of greenish-blue light. Maybe I was at the ocean and was drowning. I could hear Bruce demanding I stop squirming and screaming, but his commands seemed like they were coming from a long distance away.

The searing pain of being repeatedly struck with a whip quickly ended my attempt to disassociate from the fear and pain. It took very few hits with the whip before I did what I was told and went limp. It was at the point when I willed myself into immobility that I became aware of my ability to see through a gap at the bottom of my blindfold. At that moment it all became glaringly obvious what the situation was: my feet weren't touching the ground; I was hanging by my wrists, my feet a few inches off the ground.

JULY 5, 1981—DAY 3

Waking up startled me that day. For a brief second I had forgotten the previous two days. I felt like I was having two different sensations. Part of me hurt more than I had ever hurt in my life. It hurt to breathe, hurt to move. Every part of me hurt. And I was really cold. Yet at the same time I felt remarkably light-headed and dizzy, almost like I was floating above myself. Every part of my body from my hair to my ankles hurt, yet it felt like I was somehow oddly disconnected from it.

I was in a closet of some kind, naked with my hands tied in front of me. Not that it mattered, because it hurt too much to move to even contemplate trying to escape. Day one had been my punishment day for disobeying instructions. Day two, according to Bruce, had been my day for "in-processing." The signing of my "employment contract." A contract that I barely understood. Some of it was obvious. The contract said explicitly that I was a sex slave owned by Bruce. I would be available to him sexually anytime he desired in any way he desired. I would never deny him anything, never wear underwear, never escape and most important, at penalty of death, never tell a soul about my new status as a slave. Bruce was the master, I was the slave. My job, as I had learned in day two, was to be a submissive, a bottom, to clients into bondage, discipline, and sadism-masochism. According to Bruce, I was an actress. An actress in clients' fantasies—whatever any of that meant.

It didn't matter if I understood or not. The important thing was to do exactly what I was told and not force Bruce to punish me. It hadn't taken me long to realize that letting Bruce do what he wanted to me sexually wasn't the worst thing that could happen. Far worse was the training for what I was going to do with clients. A lot of them would want to think they killed me in order to "get off." I was the star performer, Bruce explained to me in day two. It had to look real and I better be a damn good actress or else they would do what it took to make it believable. My practice sessions with Bruce to improve my "acting skills" were far worse than anything sexual.

AUGUST 1, 1981—DAY 29

After nearly a month, Bruce decided that I looked like shit and had to get professional help because it was nearly time for me to start working. The past twenty-nine days of "training" had been a clinic for learning that absolute subservience was the only method for survival. It was twenty-nine days of torture. Mistakes were punished with a cattle prod or by being hung by my wrists and whipped. Lessons were taught in using appropriate verbiage to describe Bruce, Bruce's penis, the customers, and myself. Bruce had a very specific series of words I was to use when he was being given oral sex. I was his slave, his hole, his cocksucker . . . the list went on with far more graphic descriptions. When I failed to recite my lines in the correct order while giving him a blow job, it meant being handcuffed and anal sex. If he failed to ejaculate or ejaculated too soon, that meant a beating and the next time anal sex while handcuffed with a rope wrapped around my neck. When I didn't guess the appropriate response to a picture of his favorite porn magazine model, he educated me on what it meant to be sodomized. Bathing had been turned into a lesson on holding my breath or being anally penetrated face-first under water.

I had absorbed the information of these lessons as well as the bigger picture. Bruce could do anything he wanted to me. I had been strangled with a rope until I passed out during sex enough times to understand that my life was completely in his hands. It could be ended at his whim. The question was not so much about my life ending as it was how much pain would I have to suffer before it did. Therefore, when Bruce advised me we were going out to get me cleaned up because of the way I looked, I was under no illusions of trying to flee. My focus was entirely on trying to remember every instruction I had been given to avoid being punished upon our return home.

Our first trip was to the hairdresser in a strip mall. I was disoriented by the light of day after spending so much time blindfolded. Nothing seemed to be the right size and shape. Having been hit so many times on the thighs had made it difficult to walk. Initially Bruce had wanted me to wear a miniskirt with no underwear to the hairdresser but the bruises on my legs made that impossible. I'd have to wear the jeans I'd worn the first day. Next we would go to a department store to get me a garter belt and black stockings. So, next time, I could wear a miniskirt with no underwear without worrying about bruises showing up. And of course I would have to be punished at the day's end for creating a situation in which I was unable to fulfill part of my contract— the part requiring me to wear nothing that completely covered my vagina. Pants were illegal as they were "worse than underwear in terms of covering my hole," according to Bruce.

The first question from the hairdresser became a problem. She asked me what I wanted to do today. I had no idea and told her I had to go ask. The hairdresser looked at me quizzically when I jumped out of the chair, found Bruce in the waiting area and asked him what color. I told her to bleach it platinum but leave it long. She asked me if that was what I wanted or what my boyfriend wanted. Of course it was what I wanted I told her, but by then Bruce had taken a seat next to me. I spent the next two hours trying to conceal my fear, keep from shaking because I knew that I had made a major mistake.

On the ride back home, Bruce left no doubt as to what was coming. "How could you not know what color a slut's hair should be?" Bruce screamed at me. Making matters worse, the dye didn't take well and came out more yellow than platinum. Trying again was too risky, the hairdresser had told us. My hair was too fine to try to bleach it again that same day. Bruce decided using the stun gun on my breasts later that night would be the appropriate punishment.

OCTOBER 6, 1981—DAY 94

More lessons learned. Walking ahead of Bruce in public was a serious breach of contract; asking for Coke rather than water in a restaurant another grievous error. Slowly, though, I had learned, and the punishments had lessened. There were still the days that I was punished just because he felt like it and enjoyed it. Or when he bought something new from the adult store and wanted to try it out. But I had learned to think ahead.

Always take the option that was most uncomfortable, or inexpensive. Always drink water, not anything with flavor. Never with any ice. Always walk a step behind Bruce. Walking ahead of him was disrespectful, more than a couple steps behind was an escape attempt. Speaking without being spoken to, bad idea. Make eye contact with no one. If it was hot outside, make sure to wear clothes that made the heat worse. If it was cold, take steps to make sure I was cold. Keep my shoes on at all times so that my feet hurt when I walked.

My pain and discomfort was Bruce's goal. He seemed to be placated more often if I recognized my subservient role and inflicted pain and discomfort on myself. His belief was that I was learning my place. Learning my role. If I was obviously uncomfortable or in pain, he was less likely to inflict something far worse.

October 6 was the night of my first client. The setting: a hotel room. The client: late forties, bald, black T-shirt, pointy head. My role was to play the school girl that was "naughty," and to get spanked for doing "naughty things." The costume was a Catholic schoolgirl uniform. The role was easy. The client, Steve, was far easier to please than Bruce, and much less brutal. A few verbal expressions of how "naughty" I had been brought him to a climax and it was over. I gave Bruce the $140 money I'd made for the "show."

Bruce was pleased. His wait in the car outside the hotel had been short. We'd celebrate that night, he told me. The "celebration" was Bruce inviting his buddies over to play cards. I would be the waitress, and he would prove that he had a girl who knew her place. His buddies were astonished and excited by the sight of me letting him lift my skirt and penetrate me right in front of them without comment or any effort to stop him. At more than one poker party, a losing hand for Bruce meant another player got to "take a dip" inside me. I had shut off my feelings, shut off my emotions. Any inkling of protest on my part would bring severe punishment.

OCTOBER 17, 1981—DAY 105

On this occasion the client was different. Younger than most of the previous clients, Brian had a softness about him. Getting the money upfront was no problem with Brian. No arguments about the price. No arguments about being a working guy and deserving a break. Brian didn't even want sex. He just wanted to talk to me and try to understand what I was doing and why.

By now, the usual explanation came easy to me. Rough sex turned me on. My "boyfriend" and I needed the money because he had just lost his job as an air-traffic controller. So why not, right? Brian said I seemed young. I promised him I was eighteen. The bruises were explained by a "car accident."

Finally Brian came to the point. He said he knew Bruce was a bad guy and wanted to help me. At first, I stuck to the story. If Bruce found that I had deviated from my contract in any manner, the consequences would be severe, potentially life-threatening. But Brian sold me on the idea of risking everything to get away from Bruce. I would move in with Brian and he would take care of Bruce. The next night Brian would hire me again and we would just leave together.

OCTOBER 18, 1981—DAY 106

The whole day seemed to move in slow motion. My mind played out all the possibilities of a new life, a life with a man who cared about me. Throughout the day, I did everything I could think of to act naturally with Bruce and not give any hint of my leaving with Brian. Bruce seemed in a good mood throughout the day. Another mindless session with a client with a fetish for dressing girls as a schoolgirl that afternoon—same routine. Only this client may have been a coke addict. He was very difficult to bring to a climax. But he was the last one. So who cared? Evening came and Bruce brought me back to Brian's house. Bruce seemed elated that I had made a "regular" client.

Everything moved quickly once I entered Brian's house. Everything was set; all I had to do was tell him I was sure I wanted to leave with him and we'd go out to the car and leave. Brian told me everything was already packed, and I confirmed my desire to go with him. He told me to follow him down the stairs and out to the garage. When I opened the door to the garage reality struck. It wasn't a garage; it was some sort of recreation room. Bruce was there with three other men.

Never in my life had I seen the rage in anyone's eyes that I saw in Bruce's. His eyes seemed like they were yellow. He exploded in rage, screaming at me about trying to leave him. Within a second he had me off the ground and shoved into a corner of the room, squeezing my throat with his hands. I tried in vain to pull his hands off my throat and get my feet on the ground. Bruce was literally strangling me with his bare hands.

The room seemed to be getting brighter and I felt like I was floating. In the distance I could hear the other men telling him to stop because he was killing me. In a flash of green light I lost consciousness. A kick in the sternum brought consciousness back. My hands were tied behind my back and Bruce told me to beg him for forgiveness. Get on my knees and beg for my life. I did exactly what I was told to do.

"This was going to be a night no one in the room ever forgot," Bruce told me. He was right. I never forgot. Being gang raped that evening was the least of my worries. By early the next morning the punishment had been dished out. My voice was hoarse to the point of laryngitis from being choked and repeatedly strangled with a belt. The blood was still drying between my thighs. Electrical burns from the stun gun on my breasts and neck had blistered.

There were many more humiliations and degradations that night. Ones that taught me the absolute lesson: leaving Bruce was out of the question. I would never even allow myself to think about leaving him again. Bruce made it perfectly clear. The next time anything like this happened, it would be a repeat of this night's events except it would go on until I killed myself to make it stop. A suicide option wasn't offered this night—if it had been, I would have taken it to end the beating.

OCTOBER 31, 1981—DAY 119

It had been nearly two weeks since my escape attempt. The incident at Brian's house led to a trip to the emergency room because the injury to my throat had become infected, leading to a high fever and severe breathing difficulty. Bruce explained to the triage nurse, the RN, and finally to the doctor that he was my boyfriend and that my injury was from being mugged while wearing my purse around my neck rather than over the shoulder, and that I had stubbornly refused medical attention until this day.

I had no voice and no will to challenge this explanation. I had black tights on because Bruce feared I would be required to put on a hospital gown. There were peculiar glances at my wrists, which still had bruises from the handcuffs. That was easy to explain. I was a police cadet and being handcuffed was part of the training according to Bruce. Including being cuffed roughly so that a rookie officer would understand the feelings of the criminal. Bruce had an answer for every question.

When the doctor finally ushered Bruce out of the examining room, he asked me if everything was all right, and if not he would give me a pad and pen so that Bruce didn't have to hear what I was saying. I nodded that everything was fine. Shivering from the fever and dehydrated, I had no strength or will to explain my situation to the doctor. Instead, my fear was directed at the possibility of his mounting awareness of my injuries. But Bruce had been as charming and convincing to the doctors as he was to me the first day. A few hours later I was released.

Of course I would be punished once we got home for costing so much money because of my medical bills. But the punishment phase was apparently anemic to Bruce. Hanging me by my wrists and whipping me did little because I was too weak to react much to the pain. Instead I was limp. Oral sex was a failure because I lacked the strength to perform it on him even under threat. Apparently, even Bruce sensed he had gone too far. There were no punishments and no sex for the next two days until my fever broke.

THE NEXT THREE YEARS

For three years I was forced to let men rape me for Bruce's profit. During that time, I'd nearly been killed several times, including Bruce's failed attempt to perform an abortion on me after I became pregnant. In 1982, I entered a suburban Los Angeles hospital bleeding extensively from my vaginal area. On my wrists, ankles, and neck were burns, cuts, and scars. I had been hung from the ceiling by my wrists while Bruce shoved a broken, long-neck beer bottle into my vagina in an attempt to remove the fetus.

Fearing retaliation, I didn't communicate to the doctors what had actually transpired. Instead, I remained silent. Had these doctors given any thought to their ethical oaths it should have occurred to them that the bruises, scars, strangulation marks, et cetera, were inconsistent with attempting to abort my own child. Exactly how did I destroy my larynx attempting to abort a child? How did I self-inflict leather strap burn marks around my wrists and ankles? Since I was an inpatient for three days, why wasn't a mental health professional sent to talk to me? Why was I questioned only in the presence of my pimp who was masquerading as my older brother, pretending to help his psychotic little sister? Had I been questioned alone and placed in the psychiatric ward away from him, perhaps the outcome would have been different.

Later, I was thrown into the trunk of a car and taken across country. After being left in the trunk for long periods of time in the southwest desert in July, I became sick from dehydration. At one point Bruce took me out of the car on a remote road in the desert, handcuffed me, tied me by my neck to the bumper of his car and told me he was going to drag me until I was nothing but hair and a grease stain. This fate was guaranteed unless I agreed to remain totally compliant.

Arriving at an Arizona truck stop, Bruce pulled me out of the car, took off the blindfold and shackles and told me to walk with him into the truck stop and get a Pepsi. Weak from fatigue, dehydration, and exhaustion, I couldn't walk. I became violently ill on the brick patio of the truck stop. EMS was called to the scene. I was vomiting profusely, dirty from head to toe, and had sores on both my wrists from the handcuffs and on the corners of my mouth from being gagged for days. Did they call the police? No. They accepted his explanation about the death of "our parents" and how he was taking care of his schizophrenic little sister. Why didn't they ask questions? Why did they only treat the symptoms of heat exhaustion and not ask how I got to that point? Why did the lady getting into her Cadillac with her husband not help me as Bruce was tying my hands behind my back and putting me back into the trunk in plain view?

These incidents are not meant to shock, but to illustrate the reality of my day-to-day life. Bruce and his "clients" inflicted every torture imaginable on me, forcing me to do disgusting, humiliating things which have had a devastating effect on my mind, my body, and my soul.

In 1984, my captivity came to an abrupt end. Bruce was arrested on unrelated charges, and I was able to escape after he had been handcuffed and taken away. The police who arrested Bruce offered me no support, despite finding a young girl locked in a closet bound, gagged, and blindfolded. Even my request for a female officer to speak to was denied. The police told me that they were there to execute a warrant and that I'd better shut up or I was going to be arrested, too. I wasn't even eighteen yet.

Taking whatever money I could find in the house, I left immediately, taking a taxi to the airport and flying to the first destination available with the amount of money I had. After arriving in the new city, I found a cheap hotel and literally slept for days. The face I saw in the mirror when I awoke was hardly like the one I'd seen at age fourteen. I'd lost a third of my body weight. My once thick, long hair had fallen out in clumps and was now thin, fragile, and lifeless.

Emotionally, I was still stunned, lost in my own world, trying to readjust to a life that suddenly left me free but with no place to go and no one to turn to.

Sleep was filled with nightmares, daytime with flashbacks and raging paranoia of being located by Bruce. After three years of eating dog food and being forced to beg for it, I was unaccustomed to eating anything normal and struggled with anorexia. In essence, I still didn't exist as anything more than a slave, except I was now an escaped slave.

It has been more than a decade since then. In many ways, I've recovered, having eventually regained enough sanity to get a job and hold it. The physical injuries either healed or scarred, and I learned to compensate. But having survived this experience does not mean I have become safe from it.

Depression is still part of my life, as is shame, fear, and a strong drive for self-destruction. I still feel as if I'm crazy and fear I am a burden to my friends, a failure as an employee, and that I am destined to again be homeless, vulnerable, and alone.

There are issues I am working on towards recovery: an integral part of my recovery is speaking out about what happened to me, what I faced as a runaway teen, and what I face even to this day trying to live with the memory of what I endured. I write this story so that maybe someone who hears it will somehow be able to avoid the pain that was forced on me, and for others to know that things like I experienced really do happen—and they can happen to anyone's daughter, sister, girlfriend, niece, or wife.

As Leighton's closing line makes clear, she speaks out about her experience not only for her own personal recovery but also to alert the American public. According to a recent study published by the University of Pennsylvania School of Social Work, an estimated

*quarter million American children are "at risk" of becoming vic-
tims of sexual exploitation, including child pornography, prostitution, and trafficking. To fight this growing problem, Leighton
co-founded SE Escape, a non-profit educational organization
combating prostitution and pornography, and co-produced a doc-
umentary film on prostitution and pornography entitled* Voices
from the Underground: Survivors of Prostitution Speak Out.

Chapter Four

TRAPPED ON THE BALCONY

A TALE OF A SRI LANKAN HELD HOSTAGE IN LEBANON

Beatrice Fernando

One out of every nineteen Sri Lankan citizens—over one million people—works abroad. Of those, more than half are employed as domestic workers, primarily in the Middle East. According to one estimate, one in five women who leaves for the Gulf returns prematurely, faces abuse, receives no pay, or is forced into illicit human trafficking schemes or prostitution. Over one hundred women come home dead each year.

These women find jobs in the Gulf through employment agencies that charge them steep fees, leaving them in financial

debt and vulnerable to exploitation. They are virtually inden-
tured servants who have little recourse to fight the sexual harass-
ment, confinement, or physical abuse they often suffer in their des-
tination countries. The Sri Lankan government encourages this
exodus of migrant housemaids, sponsoring training programs and
providing shelters for women who return home with injured bod-
ies, damaged minds, or illegitimate children.

Beatrice Fernando, who went by the name of Ranga, is a
survivor of forced, unpaid domestic labor. At the age of twenty-
three she traveled to Lebanon to work as a housemaid to give her
three-year-old son a brighter future. Her story reveals the re-
markable strength of spirit that enabled her to escape a brutal
form of forced domestic slavery.

Unaware of what was about to happen, three-year-old
Samadha slept peacefully in my lap, his small mouth
slightly open, his breathing shallow and quick. Suddenly
he gasped. I wiped the perspiration from his forehead and
ran my fingers through his damp hair, then leaned over
and smothered his face with kisses, trying somehow to
make up for the two years I would be away. I had been offered a job as a housemaid for a family in Lebanon. Barla,
a distant relative of my mother's and my contact at the
local employment agency, had told me to meet him at the
airport. Nothing would be definite until Barla handed me
a passport and airline ticket, and I was beginning to worry.
It was getting late.

Sri Lanka's only international airport, Katunayake, was
dotted with May trees and coconut palms whose leaves fluttered gracefully in the light breeze. For reasons of security,
only one person was allowed to accompany a passenger inside the terminal. Everyone else had no choice but to remain

out in the open, behind a chain-link fence, while the succession of planes took off and landed.

We were seated on a bench in the shade of a May tree whose flowers carpeted the ground, their luscious fragrance filling the air. The shade offered little respite from the early afternoon sun. Tickling drops of sweat rolled down my neck, beneath my thick mane of wavy black hair. My dress was glued to my soaked back.

Twenty-three, I was estranged from my husband and had taken temporary refuge with my parents. There was one reason and one reason only that I'd decided to go to Lebanon: money. Without a college education, I couldn't find a job in Sri Lanka—at least, not the kind of job that would pay enough to free my parents of the burden of supporting Samadha and me. By some miracle, my father had raised thirteen children on the meager wages he earned as a homeopathic doctor. It had been a tough life, and I wanted more for my son than the single-room, thatched-roofed shack in which my parents lived. Samadha's toys consisted of empty cans and boxes, sticks and stones, whatever he scrounged up in the yard. I wanted him to have trucks, balls, building blocks, books, a good education, a future. After many unsuccessful attempts at finding a job, I had no option but to seek employment in a foreign land.

Barla promised me a maid's job in Lebanon that offered a salary of two thousand rupees per month, with free room and board and return airfare. In exchange I would pay five hundred rupees and sign a two-year contract. The offer sounded too good to be true. Believing my prayers had been answered, I signed the contract, and my parents advanced me the fee to pay the agency. There was only one drawback: I would have to leave Samadha behind. What could a helpless mother do other than hope it was for the best?

I looked at my watch. It was getting perilously close to check-in time. What if I missed the flight? Samadha was stirring in my lap. I glanced down at him one more time, soaking up the sight of his dark curls. It was unnatural, a mother being separated from a young child. The boy opened his eyes and, after studying his new surroundings, wiggled off my lap, ran to the nearby May tree and tried to scale it, shimmying no more than a foot up the trunk before slipping off.

Sitting on a bench several yards away and holding a black umbrella to shield him from the sun, my father calmly read his Bible. Pappa, a Seventh Day Adventist, was a deeply spiritual man who had a reputation for being otherworldly. When he walked down the streets of his village the seas would part as pedestrians stepped aside and bowed, taking off their hats. Things over which he had no control—like raising thirteen children on a homeopathic doctor's salary— didn't worry Pappa. He had no more control over his worldly circumstances than he did over my decision to work as a maid in Lebanon.

Amma, my mother, was less philosophical. Restless, troubled, she leaned against a lamp post and scanned every passing taxi.

"Barla's here!" she called suddenly, jabbing with her finger at a figure who had just emerged from a bus and was rushing our way. Turning toward the bus stop, I saw him with a mixture of relief and dread.

"Sorry I'm so late," he said, panting as he handed me my ticket and passport. "You'll be changing flights in Delhi and Bahrain. Mr. Zain will be waiting for you at the Beirut airport. Give him this letter."

My heart screaming, I gathered Samadha in my arms and once again covered him with kisses—his fat cheeks, his small hands, his tender fingers.

"Ammy," he said, "when you make a lot of money will you buy me a car?"

I pressed him so close to my chest that our hearts beat together. "When I have money I'll buy you the whole world, *putha*," I whispered. "I love you more than anything."

"Why can't I come with you?" he asked, his innocent eyes gazing into mine.

"Ammy is going far away to work for a family," I replied softly. "They won't let me bring you, my son. I'll be too busy working and I won't have any time to play with you. But I promise to write you every day. I'll be back before you know it. Until then, you listen to Chamma and Pappa and be a good boy, all right?"

Samadha wrapped his arms around my neck, rubbed his nose on my shoulder and sighed. Caressing his cheek, I walked over to my mother.

"I'm sorry you have to do this," said my mother, wiping her tears with a handkerchief. "This is not what I had in mind for you, my child, to see you become a servant. It must be your fate. How else could I accept this?"

Fate seemed like a good excuse for all of life's misfortunes, but guilt gnawed away at me. Not only was I hurting my mother, I was stealing her dignity as well. I had left my husband. In Sri Lanka, this alone was enough to bring shame upon a family. My departure for Lebanon would be more grist for the gossip mill. Poor Amma, who had worked so hard to give me a good life. . . . I would have loved nothing more than to go back home with my parents, and to let them take care of me for another twenty-three years. But how could I be so selfish? I refused to be a burden to them any longer.

"Don't be sorry, Amma," I said, kissing her. "This will only be for two years. When I return I'll have enough money for all of us, and we'll build a real house. Won't that be nice?" I smiled, struggling to hold back my tears. "You've done more than enough for me, and you still have to take care of Samadha until I return. Please keep him safe—don't let his father take him away again."

"I was only five years old when my mother sent me to live with Achchi," Amma went on, refusing to be soothed. "My grandmother made me work like a slave. Every day I had to grind one pound of dry hot pepper. When my hands burned like fire, Achchi told me to pee on my hands. I remember how awful it was to be a servant. I promised myself then that I would never do that to my children. That's why I didn't let any of you do chores in the house. I wanted you to enjoy being children, at least under my roof. But today I'm letting you go to work as a servant in some faraway household, with unknown people. How can I bear this pain?"

"You're not sending me anywhere, Amma. This is my choice, what I have to do for my child. Don't worry about me, I'll come back in one piece," I said, a lump in my throat.

"Take care of yourself," Pappa said, scooping Samadha into his arms. "Write to us as soon as you're settled."

The lump in my throat was tightening. My heart swelled with pain as I kissed my son's pouting face one last time and hurried past the chain-link fence without looking back. It was as if my spirit had separated from my body. I watched myself going through the motions—entering the airport terminal, passing through security. Then abruptly I found myself sitting in my seat on the plane, peering through the window and frantically searching for my son among the crowd behind the fence.

Where was he? Hopelessly aching for one last glimpse of him, I scanned the grounds as the plane took off.

This longing agony was so familiar—in a flash of lightning I was back on the streets of Chilaw, hysterically looking for my son, who had accompanied his father, Tilak, to the grocery store to buy candy. A couple of hours went by and I grew alarmed, thinking something awful had happened to both of them. Amma and I ran up and down the gravel road in front of our shack, questioning every passerby. No one had seen Samadha or his father.

"Amma, how are we going to find him?" I asked, trembling with fear.

"Tilak must have taken him home. Why don't you go to his mother's house and look? If he's not with Tilak, come back home. We'll have to inform the police."

I boarded a bus, forgetting that I was barefoot. Nothing mattered but finding my son. When I reached Tilak's mother's home I heard Samadha crying, "Ammy, Ammy!" Then I went inside and Samadha rushed into my arms, sobbing.

I swallowed my anger. Standing up to Tilak would only make things worse. If I roiled the waters between us and it ended in divorce, I would be ostracized. In Sri Lanka, divorce was a disgrace. So I decided to play it safe.

"Why did you bring him here without telling me?" I said as calmly as I could when Tilak's mother disappeared from the room.

"I knew you would come looking for him," my husband said bitterly. "I want you to live here with me, not with your parents."

On the plane flying to Lebanon, my fingers digging into the handbag, I tried to stay in that moment in time, wishing my son was with me once again. How could I have made this choice, knowing very well the anguish I would go through, with him so far away, for so long a time; the thought pierced my heart.

The aircraft was full. A dark-skinned middle-aged man in a coat and tie was sitting next to me in an aisle seat. His polished shoes showed no sign of dust. A stewardess was demonstrating the emergency procedure, her voice droning in my ear. When the plane cleared the clouds I looked down and my head began to spin. I rose unsteadily to my feet, praying that I would make it to the bathroom.

"If you feel sick, use this," the man next to me said, holding out a bag. "Don't try to walk now or it'll get worse. Bend over and put your head between your knees."

After filling two bags, I felt better. "Thank you," I muttered. "This is new to me."

"You look sad," he remarked. Unsettled by his remark, I stared at him suspiciously. "Sorry, I didn't mean to embarrass you," he said.

I looked out the window. Below, mountains of thick white clouds filled a brilliant blue sky and there was no sign of earth. My son was down there somewhere, far, far away. Was he crying? My arms ached to hold him. *Ammy!* His sweet voice echoed in my head. Still dizzy, now I had a headache to boot. I asked the stewardess for some Panadole, a pain medicine.

Suddenly the gentleman addressed me again, picking up the thread of our earlier exchange. "You don't have to be afraid of me. My name is Bandula," he said, and handed me his card. It read *Bandula Athukorala, Executive Director,* and listed an address in Colombo.

"My name's Ranga," I said, relieved.

He smiled. His teeth looked bright white next to his dark brown lips. "Where are you going?"

To Lebanon to work as a maid. I was ashamed to admit it. But in no mood to lie, after a moment's hesitation I told him the truth.

"Can't you find a job in Sri Lanka?" He glanced at my wedding ring. "Where's your husband?"

"You ask a lot of questions," I answered defensively. *Where is your husband?* I didn't like to think of those days gone by, when I was a bitter, lonely teenager waiting to be rescued.

I had met Tilak outside a homeopathic clinic my father opened in Marawila, a bustling town some fifteen miles from our home near Chilaw. I was helping Pappa out with secretarial work. My heart had recently been broken—my first boyfriend had ended our relationship—and I was anxious to get out from under my parents' wings. In Sri Lanka people frowned upon romance; marriages were arranged, and before the wedding day separation between the sexes was often enforced by the whip. Pappa had whipped me once simply for passing a note to my boyfriend in church. He and Amma wanted me to focus on school work—to get me to college— not think about boys. Despite their poverty, they made sure all thirteen of their children were educated.

The older I got, the more I chafed at my parents' stifling restrictions. Then one day Tilak appeared on the sidewalk outside the clinic, a handsome, curly haired man with a mustache who flashed a charming smile at me. Thirty years old, a

Buddhist, he lived with his mother and worked for a company that assembled radios in Colombo. Seeing each other on the sly, Tilak and I became fast friends.

Tilak seemed like the answer to my prayers. Though not in love with the man, I assured myself that I could love him, and within a few months we eloped. "I got married, don't try to find me," I wired my parents. We boarded a train to Bandarawela, a small town in the mountains about a hundred miles southeast of Colombo. The train huffed and puffed through a thick cool mist as it climbed the mountain, perilously close to the cliff's edge. It chugged past hills green with tea plantations, past babbling brooks that joined the humming wind in a sorrowful cry. They're mourning for me, I thought. As I sat next to this husband almost twice my age, the euphoria of freedom quickly gave way to dejection.

Taking shelter in the mountains with one of Tilak's friends, we hid from my parents. Within a few months the doctor confirmed that I was pregnant. Though I hadn't grown to love my husband as I had hoped, at the news a profound joy swept over me. A child of my own, mine to love! Stroking my belly, I made a promise to my unborn child: "I'll love you and be a good mother. Nothing in this world will ever be more important to me than you."

Tilak took time getting used to the idea of becoming a father, and when he finally did he rented an annex close to his workplace and brought me to Colombo.

From Tilak's friends I learned about the other side of my husband. Apparently his charm wasn't reserved for his wife alone. As my belly swelled and he began openly flirting with other women, it bothered me, but I learned to ignore it.

I tried to keep my marriage together, but it was impossible. Tilak began having affairs with other women, then lost his job and moved in with his mother. Samadha was two years old at the time. I rejoined my parents, who welcomed me back without hesitation.

Reluctant to go to court and gain the stigma of a divorce, I would stay married to Tilak for several more years, but for all practical purposes the marriage was over.

Startled by the pilot's announcement, I blew my nose and wiped my misty eyes.

"Of course, I have no right to ask you all these questions," the man sitting next to me on the plane continued, "but if I could prevent you from getting hurt, I'd like to try."

Hurt? "This is the only way for me to make money quickly," I stammered. "How can I get hurt doing that?"

He gave me a stern look. "Don't you read the papers? Don't you know what happens to girls who go to Lebanon to work as maids? They're abused and raped, and some are even killed. Is it worth the money to risk those things happening to you?"

Indeed, the papers had run stories about incidents like these and I had read them, but I hadn't given them serious consideration. "Are those stories really . . . true?"

"Yes!" he said, and lowering his voice added, "Don't go to Lebanon. When you arrive in Delhi, turn around and go back home. I'm going to London now, but I'll be back in Colombo in about three months. I'll help you find a job in Sri Lanka. I can promise you that."

Had I heard him right? Could I really go home to my son and have a job in three months? But why should I trust this man? "Don't ever accept help from a man," Amma had often warned me. "You'll end up paying him with your soul." I had only known this stranger for an hour—why would he want to help me? Bandula looked kind and concerned, but all I could think about was the hard-earned money my parents had paid to the agency and all the heartache I had caused them over the years.

The plane began its descent into Delhi. Nothing terrible will happen to me, I tried to reassure myself.

By the time the plane out of Delhi landed in Beirut, fear of an uncertain future had overtaken my sadness about leaving Samadha. Bandula's words echoed in my head: *Don't you know what happens to girls who go to Lebanon to work as maids?*

As I walked toward the terminal, a plane took off on the runway nearby with a deafening roar. I glanced up and watched it fly away. Maybe it was flying to Sri Lanka, I thought, longing to be in it.

At the baggage claim area, a tall skinny man who looked to be in his early forties approached me with a smile plastered on his face. His eyes were hidden behind sunglasses.

Forcing myself to smile, I opened my purse and handed him the letter Barla had given me. But the man had only one interest.

"Hand me your passport," he said.

That's odd, I thought. Why would he need my passport? I'm in a foreign land and this passport is my only means of identity, I wanted to say. But his commanding tone froze the words in my mouth. Without showing my hesitation, I handed him the document. Mr. Zain looked over the page with my photo and name and tucked it away in his briefcase.

"I have to keep it with me for now. I'll give it back to you later," he promised. "Let's go." Weary and disillusioned, I struggled along with my heavy suitcase, trying to keep up with his long strides, surprised he hadn't offered a helping hand.

His office—the employment agency, I supposed—was on the second floor in a hotel. As we entered the foyer his secretary greeted us with a smile and whispered to Mr. Zain in Arabic. She signaled me to take a seat and followed her boss across the polished floor into his office.

There were other young women waiting for placement. Greatly relieved, I looked them over and was about to ask one girl how she was faring when Mr. Zain emerged from his office and ordered us to stand in a line.

Like a frightened deer, I took my place at the end of the line, head down. A group of people, mostly women, breezed into the office. They smelled of perfume and their high heels went *tick-tock* on the polished floor as they paced in front of us, studying our faces to discern which among us would best suit them. Circling around us, they inspected our hands and feet and mentally measured our strength, health, and capabilities.

I was under the impression that I had already been assigned to a family, but here I was, standing in front of complete strangers like so much meat on a block. Never in my life had I felt so cheap and offended. Alarmed, I kept my eyes on the floor, hoping they would go away and not choose me.

A young man in his early thirties, short with a big stomach, glanced at me several times and went over to Mr. Zain.

"Ms. Suriya, this gentleman wants to take you home to his family," Mr. Zain said, beaming. He looked like a merchant who had just made a good sale.

I followed my new employer to his car. He opened the back door for me and I sank into a large, cushioned leather seat. It was so deep I could hardly see where we were going. Sitting on the edge of the seat, I tried to memorize signs and landmarks on the street.

After leaving the busy city, we came to a small town with a church on one corner, then drove toward the mountains, passing hills and valleys with sheep and goat farms.

"My name is Levi, and my wife is Beth. She'll be happy to have you," he said, looking at me in the rearview mirror.

"I hope so."

At length we reached his home. It was a two-storey house, far away from the city, up in the hills on a huge farm. When he parked the car in front of the house his wife, Beth, came to the door. I guessed her to be in her early twenties. Though slim above the waist, she had round hips and heavy legs, and she wore a kindly smile. I liked her at once.

Beth helped me up the stairs with my suitcase. "This is your room," she said. "You must be tired. Why don't you rest now? I'll show you around later." My room had an attached bathroom, its own little balcony, and a bed with two soft pillows and a pink blanket. A girl couldn't ask for a nicer room, I thought, and yet an unbearable sense of loneliness overwhelmed me.

I woke at dawn, my strength restored. After a quick shower I ventured out of my room and went downstairs. The sun was still hidden behind the hills and everyone in the house was asleep. It was a nice little home with three bedrooms, a living room, a kitchen, two baths, and a small storage room. Out in the front yard, a baby lamb played with its mother.

Later that morning Beth instructed me in my duties. "You need to vacuum the rooms every day," she said as I pulled a vacuum cleaner from the storage room.

"Please, show me how it works," I said awkwardly. I had never seen machines that cleaned floors, I had only used brooms. I marveled at the way the machine sucked up dust and bits of debris, which made tiny clinks and clacks as it passed into the bag. Beth gave me a long list of chores to complete before the day's end. In addition to vacuuming, I would be changing sheets, dusting furniture, mopping floors, and cleaning bathrooms. The windows were to be washed once a week. All this physical labor was new to me, Amma having deliberately spared me and my siblings the bulk of the housework, and a few short hours later I began to ache all over. Within a few days, however, I became accustomed to the work and was able to finish more chores with fewer breaks.

Every now and then I was asked to help clean Levi's mother's and sister's houses. The hard work kept me busy and the days sped by, but my loneliness grew. Three weeks passed without any news from my parents. Why weren't they writing to me? Impatiently, I waited. Every night before going to bed I listened to my son's voice on a cassette tape and dashed off a few lines to him. Beth had said I was not allowed to go outdoors, so once a week I handed Levi a letter to mail to my family.

One day while I was cleaning Beth's bedroom, I found some hairpins on the table, opened the drawer to put them away and spotted the letters I'd given Levi to mail home. My heart sank. Why hadn't they mailed my letters? How would my parents know where to write? My first thought was to confront Levi and Beth, but how dare I question them, my employers? Beth would think I had been going through her drawers. Unsettling thoughts ran through my mind. I quickly shut the drawer and went back to work. I'll find a way to contact my parents, I reasoned.

The workload was physically exhausting, and one morning in my fifth week I couldn't get out of bed. Beth found me curled up under the blanket, my forehead burning up. She brought me soup and let me rest. For three days I stayed in bed. On the fourth day when I returned to my duties, Beth asked me to pack my things.

"Why, where am I going?" I asked.

Beth looked at me with a worried expression. "I'm sorry, Ranga. Hurry and get dressed," and left the room.

Alarmed, I scrambled to get dressed and pack my bag. Levi came to the door and I followed him downstairs to a waiting taxi.

"Where are you sending me?" I asked him. "Aren't you coming with me?"

"This taxi will take you to Mr. Zain," he said.

"Why? Did I do something wrong? Can I please talk to Beth?" I stammered.

"We don't want you anymore," he said, slamming the door.

Before I could say anything else, the taxi took off.

Now what's going to happen to me? I wondered. Aside from being sick, I had done nothing wrong—though they hadn't paid me anything for the month I had worked for them.

The driver must have taken a different road back to the city because I didn't recognize any landmarks. I tried to talk to him but he didn't understand English.

Once we were out of the mountains he stopped the car next to a park, turned to me and rattled off something in Arabic. Assuming he was asking me for Mr. Zain's address, I tried to explain that I didn't have it but he had to take me to his office. He got out of the car, yanked the suitcase out of the trunk and signaled for me to get out. When I hesitated, he grabbed my hand and pulled me out. Muttering a few words in Arabic, he climbed back in, slammed the door and drove off, leaving me alone.

As the taxi snaked its way and disappeared into the traffic, I stood rooted to the ground, numb with fear. Slowly the noises around me started to register—horns blaring, leaves rustling, the voices of people passing by and the laughter of children playing in the park. The sunlight began to fade. People everywhere were hurrying home to their loved ones. A young couple strolled by, locked in an embrace. No one noticed me.

Soon it would be dark, and I had to find shelter. I had no money to go to a hotel and no idea how to find Mr. Zain. I picked up my suitcase, shivering, tears blurring my vision. "Please help me, God," I heard myself repeating. "Please help me."

After I'd walked about a quarter of a mile, a woman clad in brown pants and a chic silk shirt appeared a few yards ahead. She turned around as I passed and, with a curious expression, asked, "Are you lost?"

"No," I said hesitantly and kept walking, not knowing whom to trust anymore.

The woman came after me. "I'm Padma," she said in Singhalese. "Are you from Sri Lanka?"

"Yes," I nodded.

"Are you in some kind of trouble?" she asked. The concern in her voice broke down my fears. She held my hand and moved me to the side of the street. "Please don't be afraid. Tell me what happened, I'll help you in any way I can."

Comforted by her words, I asked her, "Can you take me to a police station?" I explained to her briefly what had happened.

"I hear these stories every day," she said indignantly. "It's hard to believe anyone could do this to another human being!" She paused. "I know Mr. Zain, I can take you to him if you really want."

Relief flowed through me. "Can you take me to him now?" I pleaded.

"You know, you don't *have* to go to Mr. Zain. I can put you in a good home," she said.

"But my passport is with Mr. Zain," I said.

When Padma took me to Mr. Zain he didn't look the least surprised to see me.

"There you are," he exclaimed, as if nothing out of the ordinary had happened. Padma explained to him how she had met me.

"What would have happened if Padma hadn't helped me?" I asked. "How could they send me away like that? Aren't they responsible for what happens to me?"

Mr. Zain gave me a threatening look. "You went to a good family. Why did you have to fake being sick?"

Incredulous, I stared at him. "Fake being sick?"

"Weren't you?"

"Is that what they told you?" I said. "How can I fake a fever? How can I fake dizziness?" I paused, trying to control the anger boiling inside me. "Can't you just send me back home?" I asked hopefully.

He raised his eyebrows. "Do you have the money to pay back the ticket fare?" So that was the deal. Even if I had the money to cover the airfare, I sensed, he wouldn't send me back until the contract expired.

Summoning up my courage, I said, "Who's going to pay me for the time I worked for Beth? They didn't pay me."

"Don't worry, I'll get you the money."

I said goodbye to Padma and handed her a letter to mail to my parents. "Don't be afraid," she reassured me. "If you ever get into trouble, take a taxi and come to my room or call me."

A door opened in the reception area and a tall skinny woman walked in wearing a dark blue suit, a red jacket, and a red hat. She walked purposefully over to the secretary, exchanged some words with her, then turned around and stared at me. Her face was slathered with makeup; her eyes looked big and black from too much mascara.

She went into Mr. Zain's office and I heard their voices. A few minutes later they appeared in the reception area. Giving me another hard look, she came closer and placed her long fingernail under my chin.

"Hello there, pretty one. I'm Lisha and you're coming home with me, girl. Aren't you glad?" She walked over to the secretary without waiting for my response.

"It's your lucky day, Ms. Suriya. This nice lady would like to take you home," said Mr. Zain.

Lips trembling, I approached Mr. Zain and whispered, "Can I go to another home, please? I'm not comfortable going with her."

"Don't worry," he replied softly. "She's a nice lady, a very rich woman. You should be happy to go with her."

His words failed to allay my fear, but there was no use in arguing with him so I kept quiet. After Lisha had signed all the papers, I trailed her out of the building, wondering what was to come of me. She owned a big white car. I was told to sit in front and she drove off in a hurry.

Lisha lived in a luxury condominium complex. The grounds were meticulously landscaped and flowerbeds hugged the driveway; guards stood at the entrance with rifles in hand. Lisha kept her car inside a garage on the ground floor. With a sinking sensation I got out of the car and followed her into the elevator, which took us to the fourth floor.

Her condo took my breath away. The vast space was laid with marble floors and lined with brick walls. The windows, which stretched from the floor to the ceiling, were protected from the wind by gill-shaped concrete slabs.

Fanned out of the family room from left to right were the living room (full of antiques), dining room, kitchen, four bedrooms, and a study, each with its own sliding-glass door that led to a wrap-around balcony. The kitchen had a *terrazzo* floor and ceramic counters loaded with appliances. Lisha's bedroom was a sumptuous, lavishly decorated suite with a walk-in closet.

My room, squeezed between the kitchen and the dining room, was the smallest in the house, with only enough space to hold a twin bed, a nightstand, a tiny closet, and a bureau. It had no windows and no access to the balcony. The only entrance was through the kitchen. One look at the room and I felt trapped.

With Lisha's huge home came a barrage of daily chores that made the workload at Beth's look like child's play. At least now I knew how to do housework, having been trained at my former employer's.

Hours before the sunrise, way before the birds sang their morning blues, an alarm got me on my feet. Dressed in a white uniform, bare-footed, on an empty stomach, on my hands and knees I began my chores. First on the list was to clean the balcony. I washed the walls, wiped the railings, and mopped the floor. After I finished the balcony it was time to set the table and prepare breakfast. Once the children were gone, I began to clean the family room. After dusting furniture, light bulbs, fans, pictures, and windows, I would vacuum the carpets and polish the wooden floors.

Lisha had three children: Deanna, twelve; Jamal, eight; and Jena, six. The children's rooms were the messiest, and I spent hours trying to straighten them. Each of the three children had a private bedroom with a study and an attached bathroom. Eight-year-old Jamal wet his bed every night; no amount of cleaning was able to take away the smell in his room. After changing the bedding daily, I organized their closets, polished their shoes, and cleaned their bathrooms, then ironed and put away their washed clothes.

The tasks were tedious and endless, but this was a maid's job and I hoped it would pay me enough to give my child a better life. So I scrubbed, washed, cleaned, polished, and vacuumed until my knees were numb and my muscles ached. There was no time for breaks. I ran around the house trying to complete my duties until late into the night. My goal was to impress my employer and win her heart—if she had one.

Well past midnight, after Lisha had retired to her chamber, I would collapse on my bed. But my aching body kept me from falling asleep, and just as I closed my eyes it was time to wake up again.

On my second day, Lisha came home while I was cleaning her room. I hadn't vacuumed the floor yet. Looking under the bed she began yelling.

"I haven't had a chance—" I tried to explain, but she cut me off.

"You filthy brat, don't you ever argue with me!"

Alarmed at her behavior, I decided that in the future I would choose my words more carefully. Once she was out of sight, I bent down to see what was under the bed; all I saw was a nice clean carpet.

Lisha hadn't provided me with gloves, and my hands were raw from the chemicals in the cleaning products. When I asked for some she said, "Why do you need gloves? They won't help you with your chores."

A couple of days later as I was gathering the dirty laundry, I came across a pair of blood-stained panties in the sink. I had just tossed them into the washing machine along with the other clothes, when Lisha came into the laundry room in her favorite red robe. Without makeup she looked like someone who'd had the blood sucked out of her body.

"Where are the panties that were in the sink?" she demanded.

Dear Lord, help me, my thoughts screamed inside me. "They're with the other clothes in the machine," I said as gently as I could. Her big dark eyes popped out, her ghostly face turned red, and to my horror she reached for my ear and began twisting it, pulling me toward the washing machine.

"Take them out and wash them with your hands!" she ordered.

My ear burned as she applied more and more pressure. Frantically I searched through the clothes for the underwear. When I had retrieved them, she pulled me back to the sink and turned on the hot water.

My fingers were already raw from cleaning without gloves. The burning touch of soap and hot water made me flinch, and as I rubbed the fabric against my skin I had to grit my teeth to keep from crying out.

Lisha spent most of the day away from home. Each morning she gathered the children and left. Some days she reappeared in the afternoon for an hour or so, then left again and returned with the children in late afternoon. I had no idea what she was doing, or whether she had a job. All I knew was that she was gone, and the fewer hours she spent at home, the better for me.

Day and night I prayed to God, asking Him for guidance and begging Him to watch over my little boy, whom I had not yet heard from. Having no way to mail letters, I could not receive any from him. Finally I summoned up the courage to ask Lisha whether I had received any letters.

"Letters?" she snapped. "Letters? Is that all you think about? What makes you think you are so important that I have to deliver your mail?"

Early one morning I dreamed that Tilak had kidnapped Samadha and I woke up crying. Filled with a gnawing emptiness, I wondered whether Samadha was safe, far away in Sri Lanka. I ached for my son, longed to hold him in my arms and hear his voice. I climbed out of bed and began brushing my hair, tears streaming down my cheeks. To console myself I began humming a lullaby that I used to sing when Samadha was falling asleep.

Suddenly Lisha materialized next to me. I hadn't heard her come in—she had glided in silently—and I'd had no time to wipe my tears away. Suddenly she snatched the brush out of my hand and began striking my face with it.

"Why are you hitting me?" I cried out, covering my eyes, but she didn't answer or stop hitting me until the brush broke in her hand.

"I give you shelter, I give you food, there is no reason for you to cry!" she screeched. "This is not the way to start your day. I will kill you if I ever catch you crying in this house. Now wash up and start your work in the living room. Don't go into the family room until the children are gone." She departed just the way she came in, without a sound.

That was a rude awakening for me. Not just verbal abuse, but physical. What was I to do? Wiping the blood from my face, I did the only thing I could—pray. "Forgive me, Lord, if I have done wrong, and guide me to be better. Please, Father, take care of my child, and soften Lisha's heart."

That morning after Lisha and the children left, I picked up the phone to call Padma, but to my surprise the rotary antique phone, the only one in the house, was locked. My heart pounding, I ran to the door to go downstairs and use the guards' phone, but the door was locked. It was then that I realized I was trapped. Seized by fear, I sank to my knees. Why would Lisha do this? How would I get help? What was she planning next? I ran out onto the balcony to look for anyone who might be milling around on the grounds four floors down. Nobody. With a sinking sense of despair, I dragged myself back inside to begin my chores.

Lisha hadn't left me any breakfast or lunch. I dared not touch any food without her permission. That night when I finally sat down for dinner, I found my plate piled up with leftovers from the children's plates: half-eaten flatbread and chicken skin and bones. Like a beggar from the streets I swallowed every scrap, washing it down with water.

This was just the beginning of what was to come. Like a dog sensing it is in danger, my instincts were warning me. It was clear now that danger lay ahead, and I tried to be more cautious. With no way to send for help and no place to hide, I had only two weapons, my faith in God and my love for Samadha. So I prayed each second of the day, while the image of my son's innocent face hovered in my mind. This gave me the courage to stay focused on one goal—escape.

After the hairbrush incident, not a single day went by without a knock on the head, a sharp twist of the ear, a slap on the face, or a demeaning insult, often for something as simple as a spot on the wall. With trembling hands, I wrote a note and carried it in my uniform pocket, hoping to give it to someone if there was ever a chance. "Please help me, I am in danger," it said, and underneath this message my name appeared, along with Padma's and Mr. Zain's telephone numbers.

It was not clear whether the children knew what was happening under their roof. When they were around Lisha never attacked me, and she arranged things so that the kids hardly ever saw me anyway. Once Deanna did notice the bruises on my forehead, and began staring at me. I stared back at her, tempted to ask for help, but I couldn't trust that the girl would go against her mother.

My strength was dwindling, and it wasn't only because of the abuse and grueling work. Lisha was starving me. That plate of leftovers she had left me proved to be the first of many—in fact, my only sustenance now consisted of the children's scraps. Like a dog vacuuming up the remains from his master's table, I swallowed anything in front of me. Some days I even scrabbled through the kitchen trash, filling my stomach with fish bones and chewed food.

I began searching the condo for keys to the door. Each morning I would wait for Lisha to leave, then resume my methodical hunt, looking in every drawer and cabinet that would open. Finally a set of keys showed up on the telephone stand in the family room. Heart drumming in my chest, I ran to the door. One by one I tried the keys, my hand shaking. The final key on the chain slid into the hole—freedom at last! But it wouldn't turn. After jiggling it to the left and the right without success, I began to apply pressure, turning it as hard as I could until the shaft simply snapped off.

With a sense of doom, I stared down at the jagged shard of metal in my hand. Lisha would be enraged. The shaft, wedged in the keyhole, wouldn't budge. After grabbing two steak knives, I managed, after many long, grueling minutes, to extract the broken piece. Relief flooded over me as I collapsed on the floor, bathed in sweat.

But delayed punishment was all I could hope for. Inevitably, Lisha found the broken key, and her discovery was followed by a merciless attack.

She waited until the children went to bed to confront me. "Did you think you could run away from me, you rotten brat?" she cried. "Do you think I'm that stupid?"

After slapping my cheeks until they were numb, she grabbed me by the hair and dragged me to my room. Then she shoved me to the ground and began kicking and banging my head against the ground. When I tried to fight back and protect myself she just grew more violent. The only solution was to give in. She delivered one last kick and spat on me. Then she was gone.

I lay on the floor, my head bursting with pain, my ribs aching as if they were broken. I had no strength to get up—I could only lie there in a pool of blood. At last gathering my strength, I staggered into the bathroom and stared at my image in the mirror. Two ugly bumps had sprouted on my head, and worse, a bleeding crack.

That night Lisha ordered the guards to shoot me if they ever caught me outside the house.

This incident was only the first of many remorseless attacks. Without reason, she treated me like her enemy, striking me with brooms, pans, mops, anything close at hand. She sucked the strength out of my body. If I tried to fight back she would twist my arms and kick me in the gut. If I tried to scream, she would bang my head against the wall, throw me down, and kick my bleeding body. At times, I simply passed out on the floor.

Now that it was impossible to run away, I attempted to climb down the balcony wall. One night after everyone had gone to bed, I tied a few saris together and slipped onto the balcony. After making sure no one was around, I tied my makeshift rope to the railing and climbed over, feeling dizzy as I gazed down four stories. Bricks protruded from the side of the building. My intention was to place my feet on this series of footholds and gradually descend. Alas, the gap between each brick was too great, and my short legs couldn't even reach the first one. After climbing back onto the balcony I returned to my room, weighed down by a sense of hopeless defeat.

I waited and waited, hoping Mr. Zain would call or pay a visit to check up on me, but that never happened.

Gradually, I turned into a machine. My body no longer registered pain; I had no more tears left to cry. I got used to sleepless nights and visions of food rather than the real thing. I became attuned to Lisha's behavior, hearing her ghostly footsteps before she walked, her harsh voice before she spoke, feeling her cold hand before she struck. Helplessly, I thought of my parents. For loving me and caring for me, what had I given them? Nothing but shame and suffering. Why hadn't I listened to them and studied hard and become somebody, instead of running away with a man? Now I could comprehend a mother's pain at being separated from her child. I wept with remorse for causing Amma pain, thinking back to the moment when she welcomed her prodigal daughter back with open arms. . . .

I was three months pregnant at the time. I had no trouble with the pregnancy, but I did crave my mother. Tilak offered to take me home. He hired a taxi, but when we got to my parents' house he wouldn't let me out. "Wait here," he said. "I'll talk to your parents first and tell them that you want to see them. If they don't kill me first, I'll signal you."

Within seconds I saw Amma burst out of the house with a big smile, running toward the taxi. Soon we were locked in an embrace and she was showering me with kisses, crying, "We were so worried about you! I'm glad you came home!"

"What took you so long?" Pappa asked, pulling me into his arms.

A sense of peace settled like feathers over me. I couldn't believe they accepted me after what I had done, shaming the family by running away with a man and coming home pregnant.

The ache of guilt I now suffered was greater than the physical abuse. I missed home desperately. Once more I prayed to the all-but-invisible God, and this time I begged Him, "Please give me another chance to go back home, to ask my parents' forgiveness and to be an obedient daughter to them. I promise you, Lord, I'll make them happy." Late one moonless night, I slowly came to my senses after having been beaten and kicked. I had passed out on the floor covered in blood. With a throbbing pain on the back of my head, I crawled to my bed softly moaning, "Amma, Amma!" I longed to curl up in my mother's caring arms, hear her loving voice, feel her tender touch on my bruised body. Samadha's face flashed before my eyes and, despite my effort not to make any noise for fear of reprisal from Lisha, a whimper escaped from my lips.

I lay in bed, weak and petrified. No one was coming for me, and death was closing in on me. *Lisha is going to kill me,* I realized. It was a terrible, incomprehensible truth. My breathing was shallow, my body in shock, my heart thundering. In despair I cried out to God: "Where are you, Lord? Haven't I been tested enough?" Suddenly a jolt of rage shot through me. For the first time in twenty-three years I was furious with God, and I began to question Him, to confront and challenge Him for proof of His existence. I demanded a miracle. If it didn't happen, I vowed, I would never pray again, for I couldn't wait for Him any longer.

At that moment, I made up my mind to do the unthinkable—my last attempt to escape.

One cold, early morning before the sunrise, I slipped onto the balcony. The bleak moon was fading, the sky lighting up. A blanket of silence lay over the neighborhood—people were sleeping, and not a bird was singing. Four floors down, the condo grounds looked calm and peaceful. Holding onto the cold railing, I wondered, could this be my last moment in this world?

It had been fourteen weeks since I said goodbye to Samadha, and the memories of that day weakened my spirit. With a sense of emptiness in my core, I climbed over the railing. For the sake of Samadha and myself, I had to seize this chance. Not to die but to live. Taking a deep breath, I filled my lungs with fresh air and felt the bitter, cold wind on my skin. The cement beneath my feet was damp from the morning dew. Energy surged through my body as I turned around and faced the balcony. Holding onto the railing with both hands, my toes at the edge of the concrete, my heart racing, the blood rushing through my veins, I closed my eyes and prayed.

Then with all the force I could summon, I jumped into the air.

Fernando survived the fall. She woke up several days later in the hospital, her lower body paralyzed and most of her limbs broken. The doctors told her that she would never walk again. But she slowly regained control of her lower body and took her first steps.

With the help of people she befriended at the hospital, Fernando managed to convince the employment agency to send her home, but she did not receive any pay for her three and a half months of work. Lisha never had to pay for her crimes, other than footing Fernando's hospital bills.

Upon returning home, Ms. Fernando faced the pain of social stigma; people whispered among themselves that the "crazy woman" had pushed her off the balcony for having an affair with her husband, or that she had gone to Lebanon to become a prostitute.

In an effort to start her life anew, Fernando contacted the man she had met on the plane, Bandula Athukorala, and got a job through him. Eventually she, her son, and her future husband, Nuwan, immigrated to the United States. After settling down in Massachusetts and marrying, she obtained a B.B.A. and worked in administration while her son graduated from the University of Massachusetts, Dartmouth, with an electrical engineering degree. Fernando has since published a memoir, In Contempt of Fate, *and has become an activist with the American Anti-Slavery Group, speaking before congregations, high schools, and universities, and even testifying to the United States Congress in March*

2005 in support of the Trafficking Victims Protection Reautho-rization Act (TVPRA). The committee chairman, Representa-tive Christopher Smith (R–NJ), thanked Fernando for her policy recommendations to hold job agencies responsible for the abuse of employees, remarking "in all my years working on [trafficking] we have not focused on that." The TVPRA was passed in January 2006.

(left) Beatrice Fernando, a Sri Lankan woman trafficked into domestic slavery in Lebanon, stands outside the US Congress after testifying to the House International Relations Committee in March 2005. (American Anti-Slavery Group)

(right) Boston-area nurse Margaret Rothemich is a modern day rescuer. While providing home care for a family in 1992, she recognized that the family's domestic was being held as a slave. At great risk, Rothemich contacted local police, helped the woman escape, and even provided shelter to the survivor. She is an example of how ordinary Americans are sometimes on the frontlines of the struggle to stop slavery. (American Anti-Slavery Group)

*Every year the Mauritanian anti-slavery group S.O.S. Slaves
publishes a report on the state of slavery in the West African
country. This photo, from the group's 2003 Annual Report, features
a woman rescued from slavery. She had been born a slave, and her
parents and grandparents before her were slaves. Yet she realized
that she wanted to be free from her master's family. Now free, she
faces the daunting task of rebuilding her life as an independent
woman.* (American Anti-Slavery Group)

Burma is one of the world's most brutal dictatorships, and the military junta that rules the country forces thousands of Burmese into temporary forced labor. This mother and child are survivor refugees who have escaped to Thailand. (American Anti-Slavery Group)

Rev. Ray Hammond of Boston's Black Ministerial Alliance holds a protest sign at a rally demanding that the United Nations and Secretary-General Annan take action to stop slavery in Sudan. The UN has often failed to assist those trapped in slavery or to stand up to slave traffickers, in part because dictatorships like Sudan and China sit on the Human Rights Commission. (American Anti-Slavery Group)

American students participate in the American Anti-Slavery Group's Freedom March. Some of the best abolitionist activists are young Americans. Unlike many adults, they are not jaded, and they are moved by America's own struggle against slavery. With passion and conviction, they speak out on behalf of those held in slavery and call upon world leaders to act. (American Anti-Slavery Group)

Abuk Bak, a native of Southern Sudan, was captured in a slave raid sponsored by the National Islamic Front regime that rules Sudan. She tried to escape the government militiamen who raided her village, but was caught in a lasso and taken to a slave pen. Abuk was then sold off as a slave to a family and remained in bondage for a decade, until she finally was able to escape. Today she speaks to audiences across the United States about her experience—and has even confronted the Sudanese Ambassador to the United States demanding reparations. (American Anti-Slavery Group)

Micheline Slattery has experienced domestic slavery in both Haiti and the United States. After a harrowing journey in her native Haiti, she came to America only to find herself enslaved in a Connecticut suburb. She managed to escape and today speaks publicly about her experience in order to educate Americans about human trafficking in local communities. (Garcia and Neff Productions)

Abdel Nasser Ould Yessa was born a slave owner in Mauritania, and spent much of his childhood with black African slaves waiting on his every need. After rebelling as a teenager against his society's engrained system of chattel slavery, Yessa became a human rights activist and co-founded the organization S.O.S. Slaves. Today he lectures at universities and institutions around the world about slavery in Mauritania, including his own experience as a master. (American Anti-Slavery Group)

This woman was captured in a slave raid in Sudan. She was gang-raped by government militiamen, who slashed her chest and arms with knives when she tried to resist. Today, she still bears the scars of their wounds. But she and her newborn baby—the result of being raped by her master—are now free in southern Sudan. (American Anti-Slavery Group)

Harry Wu, founder of the Laogai Research Foundation, was held in Chinese forced labor camps for nineteen years. After enduring torture, severe illness, and near starvation, Wu now uses his freedom in the United States to advocate for those currently imprisoned in Chinese forced labor camps. (Laogai Research Foundation)

Chapter Five

LAOGAI

INSIDE CHINA'S
FORGOTTEN LABOR CAMPS

Harry Wu

The Chinese word laogai *means "reform through labor" and refers to the prison system by which the Chinese government enforces many of its judicial rulings. In the early years of Mao Zedong's rule following the Communist Revolution, the Communist Party instituted the* laogai *to suppress dissent by imprisoning those deemed "counter-revolutionary." In these work camps, prisoners labored almost ceaselessly, with little or no pay, and without a definite date of release.*

In 1958 Mao Zedong declared the "Great Leap Forward"— a national campaign to use mass labor to rapidly industrialize

China, which resulted in the death of hundreds of thousands of people even in its first year. Harry Wu, a native of Shanghai and an inquisitive university student, was arrested without explanation after a group of fellow students held a meeting to criticize and denounce him. He was promptly sent to the laogai, *and spent 19 years in 12 different camps, forced to dig trenches, harvest crops, and mine coal. He was released in 1979 after enduring torture and near-fatal illness.*

Wu, who is today the executive director of the Laogai Research Foundation in Washington, D.C., struggles to remind the world that the forced labor camps did not end following Mao Zedong's death. His organization has identified more than 1,000 laogai *camps currently in existence. The Chinese government, which considers statistics about the camps to be state secrets, has repeatedly refused the Red Cross and the United Nations access to the* laogai. *Slave laborers include common criminals but also those accused of political or religious dissent, including advocates of Tibetan independence, labor union activists, dissident bloggers, and members of the religious group Falun Gong.*

While China's forced labor camps are sometimes overlooked in discussions of contemporary slavery, Wu's firsthand testimony reveals the cruelty of the laogai. *In the following chapter, he recounts the trauma of the* laogai. *Malnourished, beaten, robbed, diseased, and often killed, the camps' prisoners were enslaved by their own government and often tortured into confessing that they deserved their punishment.*

One midnight in April 1961, an ordinary passenger train arrived at a small train station. The name of the station was "Chadian," on the Beijing-Shenyang line. International trains, special express trains, and ordinary express trains did not stop at this station; only one local train stopped here. This night, a special train engine came, spewing white steam, and, with several chugs, separated the two cars full of prisoners from the ordinary passenger train, and pushed them onto a special sidetrack.

The captains (public security cadres in charge of prisoners were generally referred to as "captains") called out an order for the prisoners to disembark; a group of People's Liberation Army (PLA) soldiers and several police dogs already surrounded the sidetrack. The streetlights on several wooden telephone poles shone dimly.

From morning till night, we'd had nothing to drink, and the *wotou* buns (steamed bread typically made of maize or red rice flour) that had been distributed the night before were long since digested and gone. All of the prisoners were dizzy with hunger. We lined up by groups for roll call and a head count. Then, group by group, we were crowded into trucks. We could not hear what the captains were talking about, and we didn't want to know. All we could sense was the truck swaying back and forth. It seemed that we were driving through open countryside, with no hills and very few trees. Occasionally, we would pass over a small slope. They may have been little bridges. We squatted on the floor of the truck bed and were not permitted to raise our heads. The soldiers in the four corners of the truck used their rifle butts to hit those who tried. We could see nothing, but we could smell the scent of the earth.

The trucks came to a gradual stop, and we were herded off. It was only then that we saw that we were surrounded by a high wall. The dirty red brick wall was at least eighteen feet high, and there was an electrified barbed wire fence on top of it. There were guard towers at the four corners of the wall, but there was no light in the towers; apparently, there were no guards up there.

"Line up in twos and stand still! Step out of line when you hear your name!" The public security cadre yelled out, "Chen, Wu Hongda, and Xhang, go to cellblock 18!"

"Wang, go to cellblock 19!"

Someone asked, "Can we have a little something to eat?"

Someone begged, "Can we have a little water to drink?"

"Tomorrow! Tomorrow! Not today. Don't make trouble! Go! Go to the cellblocks!"

"Cuff him! Put him in solitary!" The captain barked. I had grown accustomed to it.

It was dawn before we realized that this was Branch 583 in the western zone of the Qinghe Farm.

The captains at the Qinghe Farm, who wore blue cotton overcoats, came into the courtyard early in the morning, ordered the prisoners to assemble, and once again did a head count. The courtyard surrounded by high walls contained over twenty rows of houses, each of which housed ten cells. Each cell could sleep ten prisoners, who were assigned to numbered groups.

Branch 583 had approximately 1,800 prisoners, divided into twelve detachments. The twenty-plus rows of houses were in the middle of the courtyard, with the toilets, the kitchen, solitary confinement cells, and tool sheds on the periphery. Of course there were no dining or bathing facilities. In front of each row of houses there were two or three faucets. Each detachment occupied two rows of houses; each detachment had two captain's offices, one records room, and one duty room. Between the houses and the walls was an open space twenty meters wide. The guards in the towers did not permit prisoners to cross over the empty space toward the walls. In the center of the front part of the courtyard was a three-foot high platform made from bricks and clay. This was the stage used to convene farm meetings.

I was assigned to group six in detachment three. I picked up my bedroll and followed the group leader to the cellblock. There was one twenty-five-foot-long *kang*, a heated bed. The whole *kang* was supposed to sleep ten. Because there were originally only eight people in this group, they had spread out their bedrolls to sleep. Now two more people had to fit in.

"Get up! Get up!" The prisoner group leader led me in and yelled, "Roll up your bedrolls and squeeze in a bit!"

Today was a rest day, so these people were sleeping in and were too lazy to move. The group leader was a young, strong fellow. He pushed and pulled them up. But one person in the middle, with a dirty black quilt over his head, was still not moving.

"Get up now! We're rearranging the sleep arrangements!" The group leader shouted.

"F— your mother!" The man sat up, completely naked. This was the customary way to sleep in the *laogai* camps.

I took one look, and it was "Big Mouth" Xing Junping! As always, the crust was still in the corners of his eyes, his front teeth were still yellow, his hair still stood on end, and he was as dirty as ever. It had been more than a year since we had been together at the Beiyuan Detention Center.

"Hi! Old Wu, is that you?" Xing Junping grinned and shouted, "I never thought I'd see you again!"

"I've come from Yanqing!" I replied, "All rivers lead to the sea. We can't escape this circle. It was a matter of time before we would see each other."

Big Mouth Xing turned over, pushed aside his bedroll, and told the group leader, "Let Old Wu sleep next to me."

My arrangements were done.

And another new life began.

On one side of me was Big Mouth Xing. The man on the other side was Chen Ming. He was approximately my age, 23 or 24, maybe a little older. He had been arrested as an "ideological reactionary." Maybe because there were bad elements in his family, maybe because he spoke too directly and was unskilled at flattery, maybe it was just bad luck. Who knew? In any event, in those years, there were a good many "ideological reactionaries": those who complained that they didn't get enough to eat; those who said the People's communes were causing trouble for no reason; those who said food substitutes were harmful; those who said that the steel refined from the smashing of pots and pans was garbage; and those who "surreptitiously listened to the enemy's radio stations." There were also those whose misfortunes did not "come out of their mouths," but who became "ideological reactionaries" because they wrote letters or kept diaries. If the whole country was leaping forward, the *laogai* system had to leap forward as well.

Chen Ming was shorter than I, and was very straightforward. He was the kind of person who would give his life for a friend. He spoke very quietly, and his skin was very fair and smooth. He never angered or argued with others. He was originally from Fujian, and he taught geography in a high school in Beijing. *Laogai* camp rules prohibited us from discussing the details of our cases. Who knew what crime Chen Ming had committed?

"Where were you transferred from?" he asked in his Fujian-accented Mandarin.

"All of us came from the Yanqing Steel Plant," I replied.

"Oh! I've heard it's not bad there. Is it true?" he asked.

"Why do they say that?" I asked, surprised.

"There are some who spent time there who said that there's a little more to eat, because it's an industrial unit."

I asked, "What's the ration here?"

"You'll see for yourself in a little while!" Chen Ming never looked at the other person when he talked. "How much did you get to eat there?"

I said, "Two meals a day, two *wotous* at each meal."

"*Wotous! Wotous?*" he asked, "What kind of *wotous?*"

"Fifty percent sorghum flour, fifty percent bran."

Someone on my other side perked up his ears and said, "Hey! That's not bad!"

Anxious, I asked, "How about here?"

"See for yourself in a bit."

Nobody would ask about your occupation, marital status, studies, or hobbies. There was only one topic of conversation for everyone: food.

An hour and a half later, it was time to eat. Two duty prisoners came, one pulling a vat of vegetable soup, the other pushing a cart loaded with large rectangular kitchen steamer drawers. The group leaders led their groups to the courtyard, and each person retrieved his food, one at a time. Each person received one ladleful of vegetable soup, which had a few leaves of yellowed greens and was a bit salty. The other duty prisoner used a wooden spatula to carefully lift the *wotous* from the steamer drawer and move them to each person's enamelware bowl. The *wotous* were quite large, each amounting to more than two of the buns we'd had at Yanqing. They were not at all dark in color; they were shiny and white, and looked very appealing.

Chen Ming saw me looking them over and said, "This is a new invention!"

"What is it?" I couldn't figure it out.

"It's twenty percent corn flour and eighty percent ground corncob powder, which is double-steamed after mixing," Chen Ming spoke to me in measured tones, as if teaching a class of students.

Recently, the *People's Daily* had been strongly recommending the findings of a research report written by a certain scientist concerning the "double steaming method." Chinese scientists said that if the double steaming method were used, all kinds of grain, including corn and sorghum, would have more nutritional value, and would be easier for the body to absorb. The so-called double steaming method involved boiling the rice or other grain in water until it was sixty to seventy percent done, then steaming it until it became a food product that was loose and soft from saturation with moisture. The advantage was that it increased the volume of the food, allowing empty stomachs to have the sensation of being full.

These *wotous* brought me instantaneous improvement. After two meals, the next morning, the constipation that I had suffered from for months was gone. My bowels flowed freely. The other prisoners from Yanqing and I all rushed to tell each other, and they were all saluting each other with congratulations, because the sorghum *wotous* at Yanqing had caused insufferable constipation. Many of us had helped dig the lumps of feces from each other's anuses. After eating the *wotous* made from sorghum flour, the feces would not come out. It was extremely painful. The digging caused many of their anuses to bleed, but they continued to dig. It was surprising to me that the inability to defecate could be so painful. It had never occurred to me that, on top of toothaches, stomachaches, and headaches, there could also be this kind of pain.

Not more than a few days had passed when Big Mouth Xing told me, "When you go to the outhouse to shit, hold your sphincter a bit tighter. Be careful not to shit your intestines out." At first, I thought he was joking. Later, I learned that this was indeed necessary, because these *wotous* had an extreme laxative effect.

The prisoners I saw at 583 were rather different from those I had seen at Yanqing. Most of the prisoners at 583 were very weak. Perhaps most of the prisoners at Yanqing were new, like me, so they still had some reserve energy. Or perhaps it was because no matter how lousy the sorghum *wotous* at Yanqing were, they were still food.

It was here that I first observed edema. The afflicted begins to swell from his feet up, the swelling gradually progressing from his knees to his lower abdomen and then to his chest. His feet cannot go into his shoes, and sometimes he cannot even wear his pants. Bit by bit, the swelling progresses upwards. The skin swells and tightens, and it is full of water, so that it has no wrinkles, is smooth and very shiny—so shiny that you dare not touch it for fear of breaking it and allowing the water to leak out. If the swelling progresses to the chest, the afflicted becomes short of breath, and it isn't long before his "soul returns to the western sky." The captains said that these people were swelling up because they drank too much water and ate too much salt, so, out of revolutionary humanitarianism, they made a new rule at the *laogai* camp: the prisoners were to be given no salt to eat, and their intake of water was to be restricted.

The next day, the detachment went out to work. We had to dig a drainage ditch. Our tools were primitive and crude. Big Mouth Xing said if we were going to cut reeds, he wouldn't go, because there'd be nothing to profit from it. But since we were to dig ditches, he would go.

"Follow me, and you'll see what I mean," he said.

The prisoners in the detachment were driven to the rice fields, rocking and swaying all the way. When we arrived at the work site, Big Mouth Xing taught me how to do farm work, how to use less energy, and how to learn the skills to work efficiently.

Presently, I saw him digging very quickly with great effort. I walked over to him and asked, "What are you doing?"

He was following a hole in the ground, digging a shovelful at a time. "Watch! Watch!" By the time he had dug seven or eight meters, the hole disappeared!

"Shit! Where did it go? What lousy luck!" Big Mouth Xing spat and said, "Let me tell you, if you see a hole, don't pass it by. Dig along its path. If it's a field mouse hole, you'll be rich!"

Then he told me that if I found a frog or snake hole, I could find meat to eat. But mice holes were the best, because mice stored all sorts of grain. He also told me what types of plant roots and wild herbs were edible. As he spoke, he picked some and shoved them into his mouth.

I said, "You don't wash them and cook them first?"

"Look at you! The intellectual strikes again. Eat them this way. This is why we say 'unclean things make you strong' (a common rhyme in Mandarin: *bu gan, bu jing, chi le mei bing*)."

In our group, Big Mouth Xing was on an equal footing with the group leader, so his friendship toward me was my protective umbrella. Intellectuals were always the scapegoats.

Branch 583 was very unfamiliar to me, and farm work was completely new to me. Although my body was already quite weak, I remained interested. Rather than entertaining foolish ideas, it was better to find peace in the status quo. It was much better to work a little than simply dwell on my troubles.

Our detachment consisted of over a hundred and thirty people, but only some seventy went out to work. Chen Ming was one of the ones who didn't go, and the captain didn't force him. We only worked six hours a day, and there were no labor quotas. The hunger that people faced was deepening.

I was already very weak, but I still wanted to go to the fields. I liked being with Big Mouth Xing. He taught me a lot of things I didn't know. More important, there was still the possibility that I would find food in the wild.

One day after work, as I passed the cellblock of another detachment, I was shocked to discover a man named Lin. He and Shi Pan had been duty prisoners at the Beiyuan Detention Center. Duty prisoners had it good in the *laogai* camps. These men were more merciless than the public security cadres. Now his appearance was completely altered. His chin and forehead bones protruded, his beady eyes were sunken into his head, and his face was a waxy yellow in color. His feet were so swollen that he was unable to wear shoes. His back was hunched, and he was leaning on the wall of the cellblock, shielded from the wind, sunning himself. He had a filthy towel around his neck, and his blue cotton cap was buttoned very low. As I recalled, he was only around thirty! But now he looked over fifty. I would not have guessed that he would be here, much less that he would have changed so much.

I walked up to him. "Hi! Do you remember me?" I asked. He did not react. "Can you hear me? How did you end up here?"

He didn't answer. Perhaps he was nearing the end.

When I returned to the cellblock, I told Big Mouth Xing that I had seen Lin.

"He won't survive more than a few days," Big Mouth Xing said through clenched teeth. "I've known for a while that he was at 583." As he said it, Big Mouth Xing pulled back his hair to reveal a two-inch long scar. Lin had made that scar while he was duty prisoner at the Beiyuan Detention Center.

"Did you see?" Big Mouth Xing said, "He hit me as one would hit a dog. Now he will die like a dog."

"Forget about the past. Don't hold grudges." I was able to speak openly with Big Mouth Xing. I said, "What do you want to do to him? Do you still have the leisure time for that? If you still have the strength for that, use it to help me, okay? I need your help!"

An odd expression appeared on his face; as he looked at me, he looked like he was crying and laughing at the same time. He was about to speak, then stopped. Finally, he said, "All right! There's nothing more for us to say. But who from Beiyuan doesn't know him? And there's not one of them that doesn't hate him. He certainly doesn't have any *wotous* to eat. Some are likely to beat him, and others are likely to steal his *wotous*. None of that is my doing. I promise you, I won't concern myself with him, okay? But there are those who will. It's his own fault."

But Big Mouth Xing was lying. Lin was not in the same detachment as we were, so it wasn't likely that Big Mouth Xing would take care of him directly, but he had friends, and they followed his orders to steal Lin's *wotous* every few days. Where would he get the strength to resist?

A month later, three prisoners died at 583, one of whom was that man named Lin. He had once been sent by the government to East Berlin to study astrophysics. Because he fell in love with a girl from West Berlin, they escaped together to West Berlin. After thinking about it, he felt that what he had done was wrong, so he returned to East Berlin and found the Chinese embassy there. He was sent home immediately. Now both his astrophysics research and his life had come to a close. Did the girl in West Berlin still remember this outstanding Chinese scholar?

I got along well with my group leader, Little Long. Once, I told him that I had fought with a man with the nickname of "Lord of Xidan" when I was at the Yanqing Steel Factory, and when I couldn't beat him, I bit his heel. He heartily approved, and said, "Don't listen to his bullshit. 'Lord of Xidan?' I grew up in the Xidan neighborhood in Beijing, and I never heard of him. Ask around. Everyone knows 'Little Dragon of Xidan'!"

In any event, all of these people were especially fond of bragging. They loved to speak of their glorious pasts, but they never spoke of their defeats. Long also said he never "swept" (meaning to steal) or "chased around skirts" (meaning to play with women). He only fought, which was considered the highest accomplishment for that kind of person. I asked him to tell me more, and he rolled up his sleeve to show me a scar on his left upper arm. Beaming, he said, "See? Once, two gangs were looking for a pretext to fight. Both sides knew me and asked me to back them up. I looked at the situation and thought, both sides are my own people. To injure either side would be bad for harmonious relations. So I set a time to meet with the two sides and mediate between them, but in the end, I couldn't settle the matter. So I whipped out my dagger, and whoosh! I plunged it in here!" As he spoke, he gestured to show me his action at the time. "I said, 'if any of you wants to fight, I'll stab you like this!' Then the two sides made peace, and recognized me as their big brother."

These were things that I had never heard of before. Listening to them was a diversion, but, more importantly, he taught me how to work, how to secretly deal with the captains, and how to survive in the *laogai* camp.

One day, I saw him beating up another prisoner behind the cellblock.

"What are you doing? Nobody has the strength to stand anymore, and you're beating him up?" I shouted, a little bit indignantly.

He turned his head and looked at me, befuddled. He had never imagined that anyone would dare to stop him, because he was extremely high-handed, and never let anyone stop him from doing what he wanted to do.

"Do you know what he did?"

Breathing heavily, Little Long said that the prisoner had dug up several bones while working. Nobody knew what kind of bones they were. He wrapped up the bones and brought them back to the camp, filled up a wash basin with water, set up two bricks, gathered some twigs and leaves, and started a fire in a corner of the outhouse that was shielded from the wind to stew them. Someone else told Little Long that they were human bones, so he walked over and kicked the wash basin over.

"What are you doing? What are you doing? These are my . . ." The man shouted with all his might, and tried as hard as he could to grab Little Long with his hands. So Little Long beat him up.

Little Long told me, "Those bones had been buried at least two years. Do you think they're human?"

I said, "I don't know! I can't identify them. But whether they are pig bones or cow bones, if you boil them a while they can be eaten, even if it's been two years. Why would you kick them over?"

"They must be human bones. How could we?" Little Long muttered.

At that time, most of the prisoners took advantage of laboring in the fields to bring back a variety of roots, wild herbs, and bones. Then they would fill a wash basin with water and boil and eat them. People were looking for anything that could stave off hunger and provide energy.

At Branch 583, there were several plots of land that, because they were elevated a bit and the saline-alkali content was lower, could be used for early crops. Little Long still had some strength, so he was sent with several other prisoners to plant seeds. When the captain was distributing the wheat seeds, he told them in advance, "Anyone who surreptitiously eats the wheat seeds will be locked up in solitary!" Then he told everyone, "All of the seeds have been soaked in pesticide. You decide if you want to live or die!"

Little Long stole a handful of wheat seeds and brought them back, and came to me. "Hey! You intellectuals are knowledgeable. Will these wheat seeds really kill us? Is there any way to get the poison out of the wheat? Look, these are real. Help me think of a way!"

"I don't think there's any way. It's impossible," I replied.

"Then," Little Long said, "Would it work to boil them a little longer?"

"I don't think there's any point! It might be a little better," I could only say, "But you'd better not even think about it!"

But Little Long tried, maybe more than once.

The food substitute *wotous* had no staying power; human physiology had not evolved to the point where the body could digest things like wood shavings. Always remembering Big Mouth Xing's instructions, I kept my anus squeezed tight. But some people did not even have the strength to do that, so they suffered from diarrhea.

And just a few days after Little Long asked me about the wheat seeds soaked in pesticide, he began to suffer from uncontrollable diarrhea. Whether it was because he had eaten the boiled poisonous wheat seeds, I don't know. In any event, his diarrhea was terrible. I told him that he had to hang on, no matter what. I taught him not to squat fully when he went to the outhouse, but do it from a half-standing position, and squeeze his anus tight. He tried it and said, "That works, but a lot has accumulated in my stomach. It will come out sooner or later!"

"Just let a little bit go each time, don't shit wildly, or your intestines will fall out." I told him, "Be patient. Tomorrow when I go to work in the fields, I'll try to find some dry tree bark."

The next day, I found a handful of dry tree bark, and I roasted it slowly in a corner of the outhouse. When it had turned into char and ash, I made him swallow it.

"Will this stuff work?" Little Long asked doubtfully.

I said, "We have to give it a try. In any case, it won't kill you. And it might rein in your diarrhea."

On the third day, someone carried Little Long back from the outhouse. He was dirty and smelly. It turned out that he had fallen in the outhouse and couldn't get up. He died! Big Mouth Xing and I took off all his clothes and washed his body. Little Long's skeleton was thick, but his muscle tissue was all gone. His ribcage protruded and his abdomen was sunken in like a basin. The diarrhea was certainly all gone now. We dressed him in the old People's Liberation Army coat that Xing Junping had traded for a stolen chicken and a pair of my western-style pants, and he was carried away that way. Nobody knew where he was taken.

When he was alive, like Xing Junping, he had often told me how to choose wild herbs. He boiled a big basin full of them every day. Frequently, he couldn't wait for the water to boil before gobbling them up. I always told him, "No matter how dirty or cloudy the water is, as long as it boils, you can drink it. No matter what you eat, you must let it boil to kill bacteria!"

But these words did not stop death from summoning him.

There seemed to be a pattern. The stronger a person was, the less able he was to withstand hunger. In the detachment and on the farm, most of those who died were strong young men or the elderly, who were like candles in the wind from the start. It is probably because people with strong bodies had greater demands. The likelihood of disease is also increased when hunger drives a person to eat indiscriminately. At the time, the captain always said, "This is not death from starvation. This is the result of 'eating indiscriminately.' The Communist Party does not starve people." Indeed, the causes of death were always ordinary illnesses such as cold, flu, fever, or gastroenteritis and diarrhea. Nobody had any resistance to disease then. Who ever heard of the Communist Party starving people?

In the spring of 1961, the Central Committee of the Chinese Communist Party made a new decision concerning labor re-education. Every person who underwent labor re-education would have a "term." They did not use the word "term of imprisonment," because the communist government always said that labor re-education was a "supreme administrative punishment," so it did not involve any legal measures or judicial procedures. These people were not considered "criminals." Rather, labor re-education personnel were referred to as "classmates." The new rules set a minimum term of six months for labor re-education, with a maximum of three years. But if one's behavior was bad, upon expiration of his term, the public security department had the right to extend it.

The so-called "labor re-education term evaluation campaign" required each person undergoing labor re-education to report his class origins, personal origins, the facts of his crimes, and his performance since labor re-education; such reports were made at both the group and the detachment levels. The group "classmates" would review the reports and propose how long each individual should undergo labor re-education. Then the reports were submitted to the detachment, and, a few days later, everyone's labor re-education terms were announced. Herein lies the essence of the Communist Party's art of governance, referred to as "from the masses, to the masses." Self-assessments and public discussions were held until each person became genuinely convinced. The Communist Party had implemented democracy not only among the people as a whole, but even among the targets of its dictatorship. They would lock you up or kill you, and still demand that you be utterly convinced and laud the decision loudly. The campaign proceeded vigorously, and all of the "classmates" became the targets of education efforts. At the time, virtually all those with rightist and counter-revolutionary cases were given the maximum term of three years. Moreover, all of the terms were to be calculated beginning from May 24, 1961. No discount was given for time previously served.

I did not concern myself much with this campaign; because I had only been in the system a little over a year, I remained unable to adapt to the reality of hunger that I faced daily, and had no time to bother with the terms. Additionally, at least I had a deadline, three years. With something to look forward to, it seemed that a bright light had appeared in my tunnel of life.

Little Long died at the end of July, which was my third month at Branch 583. When he died, the captain appointed me as group leader. In fact, this was meaningless; group leaders did not receive additional *wotous*. Besides, a month later, malnutrition had rendered me unable to stand.

One day, we went out to labor. Another prisoner in my group who was off to one side shouted, "Quick! Come see!" He had discovered a hole in the bank of a drainage ditch. One look at it immediately called to mind what I had learned from Big Mouth Xing, and I determined that this was a treasure trove.

I grabbed the shovel from his hands, and, with some un-known source of strength, quickly dug in, following the hole. The hole went up and down for a full six or seven meters. Based on the contour of this hole, I was certain that it was that of a field mouse. Then I discovered some grain husks, and I knew that I was approaching the mouse nest. I stopped suddenly, turned to the other prisoner, and said, "Go away. Go! Get out of here!"

"Why?" He, too, became fierce. "I found it! It was I who called you here. You helped me dig, so I can share some with you!"

Without the slightest hesitation, I took one step back, then summoned all my strength and punched him. He fell onto the bank.

"Big Mouth Xing!" I shouted. "Come here, quick!"

When he heard my call, he bounded toward me.

I said, "Get him out of here!"

Without a word, Big Mouth Xing grabbed his legs and dragged him off to one side.

My eyes may have popped with greed at the time. After only two more shovelfuls, I had arrived at the mouse nest. The nest contained something like two *jins* (one *jin* is approximately one pound) of corn and two *jins* of soy-beans, every grain of which was round and plump (the mouse had a keen eye!), and over a *jin* of rice in the husk, but no wheat. I wrapped all of it up in my jacket, tied it around my waist, and, with Big Mouth Xing escorting me from behind, I returned to the cellblock. We placed this package between his pillow and mine, and in the daytime, no matter where I went, I took it along with me, to guard against theft.

For almost two weeks, every day we boiled a meal. I made it into a big basin full of thin porridge, and shared it with Big Mouth Xing. I also gave Chen Ming a small bowl each time. No one dared try to grab it, because Big Mouth Xing was standing guard.

I wanted to give a bowl to the man who had found the hole.

"No way! Don't give him any." Big Mouth Xing stopped me, and said, "One look at him and I get angry!"

I said, "Why? Why make enemies? Besides, he was the one who found the hole in the first place!"

Big Mouth Xing said, "What do you mean, enemies? Surviving is everything! You do as you please!"

"He deserves a share," I insisted.

"Then why did you clobber him at the time?" Big Mouth Xing asked.

I had no response to that. I paused a moment, then said, "Forget it, give him a portion!"

Big Mouth Xing said, "I'm not saying that you absolutely should not give him any. I just hate his kind of person; if one of them dies, it's one less to deal with."

Amazed, I asked, "What do you mean?"

"Do you know why he's in here? You won't believe it when I tell you. He sells his ass, but he looks like a man. What the heck is that?"

"How do you know?" I asked.

"The day he entered the detention center, he confessed it in the study class," Big Mouth Xing replied confidently.

A bit ignorantly, I asked, "Is this a crime too?"

"Of course. Think about it. If all the men in the world were like him, what kind of world would it be?" This was Big Mouth Xing's opinion. "I just hate this kind of person." Big Mouth angrily ended the conversation.

Homosexuality violates the moral standards of communism. It is a crime. In this respect, the viewpoints of the communists and the German Nazis are the same.

The original system of food distribution—whereby the duty prisoner was responsible for retrieving the detachment's food and distributing it to each individual—was no longer practicable after an incident in which our detachment's food was stolen. The duty prisoners had also begun to steal, and were no longer reliable. The branch issued an order to change the system. At each meal, the captains were assigned to stand at the door of the kitchen, one at a time, in shifts. According to a prearranged sequence, and led by the group leaders, each group went together to the designated window in the kitchen. First, the detachment and group numbers were reported, then there was a head count. After this information was verified, each person retrieved his own portion and returned to the cellblock to eat.

The more desperate the hunger, the crazier people became. Once, I had just received my ration—one large, white *wotou* and one ladleful of vegetable soup—and had turned around, when a prisoner grabbed my *wotou* and ran away, shoving it into his mouth as he ran. I shouted and chased him, but when I caught up with him, he had already swallowed the *wotou*. I was so angry, I wanted to beat him up, but what was the use? There was no way I could get my *wotou* back, and hitting him would only waste my energy. I lowered my head and left.

When I returned to the cellblock, I told my group, "As long as I am here, this will never happen to our group again!"

Each time our group went to the kitchen, we went together and returned together, to protect each other. But one time, three people partnered to steal Chen Ming's food. One person grabbed it while the other two protected him. After the incident, I led Big Mouth Xing and the whole group to find those three people. We surrounded them and beat them until they no longer had the strength to cry "mama."

The stealing and fighting were constant. The fights were not ferocious, because nobody had any strength. Even I gradually learned how to fight. Naturally, I didn't have the strength to swing my fists as beautifully as I had seen in the American movies. But I knew that the first slug had to seal the opponent's eyes shut, so it had to be aimed at the nose.

The farm's outhouses bustled with excitement. People did not eat much, but the frequency with which they ran to the outhouse was high. The outhouse served another function—the cooking of food. The outhouses all had three brick walls and thatched roofs. There was a four-foot-high brick wall blocking the front. Inside, there were rows of six or ten urinals made of cement. These places were shielded from the wind and it was easy to escape notice. So there was always somebody carrying a large wash basin and a bundle of twigs under his arm to the outhouse to start a fire and boil food. Even if someone was defecating nearby, they did not disturb each other. The wash basins served multiple purposes.

Besides cigarettes, the other marketable commodity at the time was salt. Apart from these, nothing—not clothes (even those made of real wool or leather), not books, not other commodities—had any value. According to the captains and the prison doctor, salt was the cause of edema, so we were given no salt to eat. But how can people go without salt? Thus, we employed all possible means to find it.

There was a prisoner named Niu Zhenhe. He was a Muslim. When he wrote home asking for clothes, shoes, and socks, he inserted the following line: "Need NaCl." Because most of the captains only had an elementary school education, they did not know what "NaCl" was. At the time, as long as a letter did not ask for food such as fried flour or pastries, it could pass the censors. Niu Zhenhe's parents were puzzled. What was NaCl? Their daughter, who was a high school student, realized what it was. NaCl is the chemical formula for salt. When family members came to visit him, they secretly handed him a package of salt, which became his store of a rare commodity from which he could profit handsomely. The prisoners gathered wild herbs and tree roots in the fields, which tasted terrible without salt. So they traded the wild herbs that they had obtained with him for salt. Niu Zhenhe became "influential." Nobody knew how much salt he had, and he never let anyone see it. He kept the salt tied around his waist in a cloth pouch. After the terms of a transaction were set, he would run off by himself to a secluded place and pour out a bit of salt—perhaps one or two grams—onto a sheet of old newspaper, to exchange for the wild herbs or other similar things. Later, others became greedy, and a group of people beat him up and robbed him of his salt. In fact, it was really pathetic—it was said that he only had a handful of salt left.

One day in early July, Big Mouth Xing suddenly said to me, "I want to discuss something serious with you. Before I say what it is, I want to make clear that you must be dependable. You have to understand, it is only because I respect you that I came to you. Are you willing to escape with me?"

He was a little uneasy, because this topic was absolutely off limits in the *laogai* camps. I started to speak, then stopped. It was very difficult to answer him. I understood that Big Mouth Xing trusted me, and I didn't want to disappoint him, but I had never believed that escaping was a smart thing to do. Big Mouth Xing saw that I felt awkward, and he said, "If we die, we die outside, like real people. What kind of life is this in here?"

"Where would we go? Where could we stay? Where would we find food? By robbing? By stealing?" I said, "We could survive today, and maybe tomorrow, but how many days could we survive?"

"No matter what, I do not want to continue to live this way," Big Mouth Xing said.

"Even if I went with you, and even if we had no concern for the next step, I think neither of us has the strength to make it out of the 583 area. Even if we made it out of 583, I'm afraid we wouldn't make it out of the Qinghe Farm area. I don't think I can walk very far," I answered gloomily.

Since the day I was arrested, thoughts of escape had never ceased. I often thought of the misfortunes of the main character in *The Count of Monte Cristo,* and remembered from novels that I'd read and movies that I'd seen how to jump over walls and cut barbed wire fences, how to dig tunnels, how to run by night, and how to get rid of the hounds on the chase. This situation was different from any situation ever written in a novel because communist prisons are different. Even if I made it out of the *laogai* camp, where could I go? Perhaps the proper thing to do would be to return to my father's side, but if I went home and my parents did not take me to the police station, they would be finished. How could I do that to them? In communist society, there was nowhere to turn.

Big Mouth Xing hung his head and remained silent. I had never seen Big Mouth Xing cry, but now I saw a teardrop roll down the side of his nose. I was sad, too, whether for him or for myself, I wasn't sure. I was very, very sad. We no longer had any options available.

It wasn't long after that Big Mouth Xing encountered the same kind of diarrhea that had afflicted Little Long. In those days, he was particularly full of bluster, shitting his brains out on the one hand, and eating ferociously to make up for it. But the more of those grasses and wild herbs he ate, the worse it became. So, like a madman, he looked for opportunities almost every day to rob others of their *wotous*. But those *wotous* made from corncobs had been the source of the problem in the first place.

One day, a batch of packages that family members had sent to prisoners arrived. In the middle of the night, he broke down the detachment office door and tore open each package, looking for something to eat. Later, the captain announced that he was to be locked up in solitary confinement. This had already become a very rare occurrence, because when the weakened were sent to solitary, the majority of them died.

"No! I won't go! No!" Big Mouth Xing yelled, terrified when he heard the word "solitary." "Do anything but send me to solitary. I won't do it again. Please, I beg you. Have mercy this once. I will absolutely not rob or steal again. Mercy! Give me one more test!"

Big Mouth Xing went down on his knees and begged the captain for mercy.

The captain said, "Send him to solitary. This is not the detachment's decision. This is an order from the branch office." Stealing packages sent by family members was a serious matter.

"I swear, I will not steal again. Don't lock me in solitary!" He grabbed a shovel and ferociously chopped off the little finger of his own left hand. "My bloody finger is proof of my . . ."

The captain had no choice but to order someone to take him to the prisoner's dispensary to have it bandaged, and he escaped going to solitary confinement.

Big Mouth Xing died two weeks later.

During those days, if anyone had a scratch or cut, only a tiny bit of blood would flow—primarily a translucent yellow fluid—and it was very difficult for wounds to heal.

When Big Mouth Xing cut off part of his finger, he shouted "F— your mother!" and threw it over the wall. It was as if part of him were now free. The flesh in the finger wound was gray in color, with the bone sticking out. The wound never closed. All the prisoner doctor could do was apply a packet of sulfanilamide powder every day. By the second week, Xing Junping was crying out in pain, shouting loudly. The captain came to look at it, and ordered the prisoner doctor to give him a painkiller, but it had no effect. Xing Junping began to suffer from a high fever. Hot to the touch from head to foot, he spent the day speaking gibberish, shivering and cursing, "F— his mother! F— his mother . . . !" These were the only words he could use to fully express his feelings.

I could only stand by and watch. There was nothing I could do for him. In the final two days, he was no longer able to eat. Already semi-conscious, he told me, "Old Wu, you eat it . . . I can't . . . you eat it!"

How could I eat this portion of food?

One day later, he breathed one last "F— his mother!" and died. He had come into the world with nothing, and left it with nothing as well. But he left his own words, "F— his mother," as a curse on the entire world.

Though Wu would endure many more years in the laogai, *he did not lose his desire for justice. Mr. Wu was released from the* laogai *in 1979 and came to America in 1985 to be a visiting professor of geology at the University of California at Berkeley. In the early 1990s, he left academia to devote himself to exposing human rights abuses in China and established the Laogai Research Foundation (www.laogai.org).*

China's rapidly growing international trade means that lao-gai *can internationally export their products including socks, green tea, paper clips, and even diesel engines. Wu's organization reports that the Chinese government actually grants special privileges to prison camp enterprises as their cheap labor attracts foreign investment and sales at the same time as it benefits the central and local governments themselves. Wu has helped CBS, ABC, BBC, and* Newsweek *expose the import of slave-labor goods from China and advocated for US Customs Service action to block import of* laogai *products.*

In 1995, Wu was arrested as he tried to enter China. Convicted for "stealing state secrets" and sentenced to 15 years in prison, Wu was instead expelled from China following international pressure. In 2001, 2002, and 2004, he was nominated for the Nobel Peace Prize. In 2003, the word "laogai" was added to the Oxford English dictionary.

Nonetheless, millions of people continue to suffer inside the laogai, *and more are sentenced to the camps every day. Wu's work challenges governments and human rights organizations to do more to help stop this massive—yet often overlooked—form of modern-day slavery.*

Chapter Six

OUT OF EGYPT

A LIFELINE VIA EMAIL FOR
AN ENSLAVED AU PAIR IN CAIRO

Selina Juma

*The world's best-known slavery narrative is the book of Exodus'
account of the Israelites' bondage in Egypt. The biblical precedent
of enslavement and redemption along the waters of the Nile
River strongly inspires Selina Juma, whose modern-day slave
narrative follows. Juma's story is decidedly contemporary: she first
met her eventual slave masters through a website and she was ultimately rescued thanks to an international email exchange.*

*Juma, who grew up in Kenya, sought work as an au pair, and
through an online match site found employers in Egypt. But upon
arriving in a posh Cairo neighborhood, she discovered that what*

sounded like a good job offer was instead domestic servitude. Her story does not feature the levels of brutality as some others in this collection, yet it represents a form of human bondage that traps hundreds of thousands of people around the world today.

Juma's story may be the first slave narrative to include email excerpts (the direct quotes come from emails in Juma's Yahoo! account). It also demonstrates that rescuers can be ordinary Americans, sometimes merely sitting at home at their computers. Indeed, if her friend Ellen had not been aware of contemporary slavery, Juma might still be held in bondage.

This account, composed by Juma after she returned to Kenya and edited by writer Avi Steinberg, reveals how Juma drew on religious inspiration to survive her ordeal. She also offers keen observations—"realizing that I was in bondage was the first stage of my liberation" is one example—that provide timeless insight on the slavery experience.

For most of my life, slavery was an exotic concept to me. I associated it with the Israelites' bondage in the land of Egypt, as recounted in the Bible. To me, slavery was about mythical lands and the clash of great peoples; it involved searing oppression on a grand scale and divine wrath. I imagined throngs of people bent in labor under taskmasters' whips, as in the movies. I thought of Pharaohs, of princes and princesses. Slavery happened on an epic scale.

My own encounter with slavery, however, was not epic. It was, in fact, very common. Mine is the story of a regular person groaning silently and anonymously—like many other regular people around the world—in the darkness of her own personal Egypt. My bondage was not imposed by royal decree. Instead, it came about so quietly, even I didn't notice it creeping up on me. It began with the simple click of a mouse.

My life wasn't spectacular. Like most people, I struggled constantly to keep up with my bills. My parents were aging, and it was getting harder for them to work. My father, a foreigner in Kenya, could not work legally in the country. At twenty-six, I alone was responsible for their welfare, for myself, for my nephew's school fees, and for the needs of my brother, a drug addict committed to a mental institution. My bills were piling up and my debts increasing.

Then disaster struck. The September 11 terror attacks in the United States had social and political consequences around the world. The travel industry in Kenya, where I was employed as a reservations clerk for a Somali airline, was hard hit. Cutbacks led to layoffs and I soon found myself without a job. My debts continued piling up, and I was getting desperate.

I felt I had no choice but to look elsewhere for my work. Like many women in Kenya, I searched for an au pair job abroad. I remember thinking: "If only I could find a job as an au pair, everything would be fine. If only, if only, *if only* . . ." This feeling took the form of a prayer in my heart. Every Sunday I would go to church and put this prayer into speech: "I don't ask that you take care of all my problems," I said to God. "I ask only for the chance to resolve them myself." After church, I would go to the cyber café to await His answer. I did this week in and week out.

One day it came. A nice American woman named Ellen was looking to hire an au pair. We exchanged friendly emails but, as it turned out, she wanted to hire someone closer to home. At the time, I was very disappointed that things hadn't worked out. Only later did I realize how this chance connection with Ellen would play a large role in my salvation. God answered my prayer again and another job possibility popped up. I received an email from a woman in Egypt:

Dear Salina, [sic]
Thank you for sending the pictures so promptly. You have a kind face which is what I need for my daughter. You will be required to take great care of her and to do daily house-cleaning such as vacuuming, etc. You will have your own toilet and sleeping area. If you are willing to stay a minimum of 2 years with us (we hope to be like your family), then write back so we can move to the next step.
Best Regards,
Mrs. Rahim

This was exactly what I had been hoping to hear. I consider myself a kind-hearted person, and Mrs. Rahim seemed to recognize this quality in me. I took this as a good sign. Not only was this the kind of work I was seeking, but Mrs. Rahim's attitude seemed perfect to me. Many people had been warning me about the dangers of working abroad—of the bigotry and isolation I would encounter. But Mrs. Rahim's offer to "be like family" warmed my heart. I also felt more comfortable staying in Africa and believed that this might be another bond of kinship.

I wasted no time. I rushed back an email accepting the job and delved headlong into logistical questions. Apologizing for proceeding so quickly, I explained in another email that "you seem to be the kind of people I would love to work for." God seemed to have answered my prayers.

We agreed on a salary of $150 per month. In our emails over the next few months, Mrs. Rahim often reassured me by saying that she was looking forward to welcoming me into her family. She promised to pay for my return ticket to Kenya as a "gift for your services." In that same email, Mrs. Rahim wrote, "Don't worry Salina, we are a very good family and we need someone who is honest and hard-working like you. I hope we will be happy together."

But she wasn't always friendly. If I didn't respond to her emails immediately—which was the result of the dozen obstacles that separated me from Internet access—she quickly made angry accusations. Even though we emailed often and I responded to her requests as promptly as possible, she repeatedly accused me of "lacking sincerity" and threatened to hire someone else.

Although this type of talk bothered me, I forgave her ignorance and prayed for God to forgive her. How was she, a wealthy woman, supposed to understand the circumstances that would drive a person to leave her home, her church, her country, and her family? How could she understand the pressures that would cause a person to leave everything in order to save their family?

Whenever I replied to her email with news that I had accomplished the various tasks she requested—seeing doctors, buying a plane ticket—her kindness was restored. She would return to talking about how excited she was that I would be joining her family. Although these shifts between warmth and hostility seemed strange to me, they could also be explained by the awkwardness of email correspondence.

Since I didn't have the funds to purchase a ticket to Cairo, I was forced to borrow yet more money from friends. I was nervous to start my journey deeper in debt, but excited that I would soon begin to pull myself out.

Sitting on the Egypt Air plane, ready to take off, I finally had some time to collect my thoughts. I recalled the endless hours of emails, medical examinations, lines at embassies, filling out documents, and praying. I thought of all the people who were relying on me: my aging parents, ill brother, young nephew, and the friends who had lent me money. I felt as though they were all there with me, and I was comforted by their presence.

Although I had worked in the airline industry, I had never actually stepped on a plane. After an exhilarating liftoff and a rapid ascent—I couldn't believe how quickly the plane left the ground—I got my first aerial view of my homeland. I could see the soaring towers of downtown Nairobi give way to bands of neighborhoods and to vast, sprawling slums. Everything seemed so serene, so neatly ordered. I thought of how distant the complications of the human world must seem to God.

After a long flight and car ride from the airport, I finally arrived at my new home on Ramses Street in the Cairo neighborhood of Heliopolis. The neighborhood was fancier than any I had ever seen. The streets were lined with beautiful villas, luxury cars, and posh hotels. Egypt's president had a palace nearby.

I was exhausted and anxious: what would my new "family" be like? I was nervous to be so far from home and wondered how long it would take for this family—and especially Mrs. Rahim—to accept me as one of their own. But as soon as I walked through the door, my life changed in ways I never could have imagined. I was told to put my bags down and take a shower before meeting Mrs. Rahim. Our first meeting was impersonal and businesslike. My new boss acted as if I had just come to her from down the street and not half a continent away. This was not the family welcome that I had been promised. I was put to work immediately.

Although my flight had left Nairobi at 4 A.M. and the trip had exhausted me, I wasn't permitted to rest for even a moment. As each hour passed during that first day—a day full of directions and chores—my heart sank. I wanted to do a good job and make a good first impression, but my body was giving way. And I felt insulted that the family had not recognized my long journey. Finally, in the evening, the family cook gave me a chair next to the clothesline and told me to sleep. Even though it was very uncomfortable, I immediately fell asleep.

Throughout my time in Cairo, the cook (who was Arab like the Rahim family) became the closest thing I had to an ally. Although her loyalty was first and foremost to her employers, she gave me much-needed guidance. One of the first pieces of advice she gave me was: "Be very careful with Mrs. Rahim. She is very protective of her daughter. She loves her more than she loves her husband—and maybe even more than she fears God."

The cook also advised me on the rules of the home. I was told to wear a maid's outfit at all times and never don my clothes from Kenya. In accordance with Islamic law, I was to keep my head covered, even though Mrs. Rahim herself went without a headscarf. I believe that this measure was taken to humble me not before God, but before Mrs. Rahim—to remind me of my position in the world: a penniless nanny.

There were other rules as well. I was never to leave the home, nor speak to anybody. I was to wait in the kitchen for the family to finish its meals; I was only allowed to eat their leftovers. I was not permitted to sit on their chairs. My email use was limited to fifteen minutes a month. I was not allowed to attend church.

Although Mrs. Rahim had promised a private sleeping area and bathroom during our email correspondence, the only bed I got was a mattress next to the dining room table. The family gave me no privacy. I wasn't allowed to lock my closet and it was routinely checked.

Every facet of my life—large and small—was controlled by Mrs. Rahim. She would accuse me of using toiletry items too quickly and punish me by not replacing them as they ran out. For an entire month I had to use toilet paper as a substitute for maxi pads. This was especially stressful because I was given only enough toilet paper to last for three weeks—if I ran out before that time, Mrs. Rahim would punish me.

I lived in constant fear and stress. I prayed every day and read the Bible, but even this became a source of agony. Mrs. Rahim would see me reading and accuse me of insincerity, saying that I wasn't really reading, that I wasn't a real believer.

The worst part of my situation was that my fate was entirely in the hands of the family. Not long after I arrived, Mrs. Rahim had come to me with a request.

"We need your passport, Selina," she said.

"I'm not sure," I replied. "It's my main legal document."

"Trust me, Selina. We've done this before. It's for safe keeping."

But still I hesitated. Two days later a doctor came to check me out. Mrs. Rahim didn't trust my doctors in Kenya and was forcing me to redo the entire battery of medical exams and tests. The doctor's visit was used as a pretext to get my passport—I was told that they needed my passport in order to document something for my medical records. But they didn't return it to me.

Without a passport, I was completely vulnerable. And since I didn't have a work visa, I could be turned in to the authorities. The thought of being handed over to the Egyptian police without any documentation sent shivers down my spine. At various points throughout my time in Egypt, Mrs. Rahim threatened to do just that. Having no passport also meant that running away from the Rahims' house was not an option. The family could do with me as they pleased.

Despite my difficult circumstances, I believed that I was strong enough—in body and soul—to tolerate the harsh treatment and abuse. I tried to remain focused and remember that it would all be worthwhile once I received my money. Every day I told myself that the sacrifice was worth making.

The days, however, passed by slowly and painfully. In Cairo, dust swirls all day, blanketing everything and everyone. It lays its claim on everything, big and small, and finds its way into every corner. If you stand around too long, you'll find dust in your mouth and hair. My job consisted of waging a futile war against the Egyptian dust.

Each day began at 6 A.M. with a thorough dusting of the chairs and plants on the balcony. From there, I dusted and scrubbed the salon: tables, chairs, endless silver, pictures, lampshades, six carpets, and a large mirror. Last came the floor—and a throbbing backache.

Then I scrubbed down the laundry room, the sliding doors, kitchen sinks, counter, oven, and again, the floor. Throughout the day, I toiled under the watchful eye of the cook, who—looking out for her own interests—kept to her strict orders to prevent me from taking a break.

At 8 A.M., Mrs. Rahim's daughter's morning would begin. I would wake her up, wash her face, brush her teeth, sit her on the toilet, and wash her backside. After making her breakfast, feeding her, and clearing the table, I proceeded to clean her room, dust her pictures, make her bed, and clean the floor.

She was a stubborn and spoiled child who, even at age five, could do nothing to take care of herself. She was raised to believe that the world was created for her and that she was my boss. She treated me accordingly, mimicking her mother's abusive behavior, while adding her own childishly cruel twist. I walked a thin line with the child, afraid of incurring her mother's wrath.

After dealing with the child, I had to clean the bathroom, a disgusting job that I had to do with my bare hands. During my time with the Rahims, I endured many abusive epithets, including being called "black monkey" to my face. Yet, if anyone displayed crude behavior, it was this family. They appeared not to know how to use the bathroom normally—and I had to clean up the mess.

The rest of the day was spent dusting and scrubbing the TV room, from the carpet to the artificial flowers and everything in between. Then came the master bedroom and, at 2 or 3 P.M., I had to feed the child again, though she often refused to eat unless her mother was present. Following the meal, I played with the child. Because I was "black and dirty," according to the child, I was unfit to touch her toys or teach her anything.

At night I cleaned dishes, scrubbed down the kitchen, removed the rubbish, and took a shower (I was not permitted to shower in the morning). I tried to be in bed by 10 P.M.; if there was company, this was pushed back until 12:30 A.M., for I was expected to clean their dishes and tidy the kitchen before bed. In any case, I couldn't go to sleep until the living room—which served as my makeshift bedroom—was clear of people.

In a matter of weeks, my schedule changed for the worse. I was expected to wake up at 4:30 A.M. to begin my chores. Often the child would awaken at 6 A.M. and demand my attention. When the family gathered for large meals, often on Saturdays, I was expected to work even harder. I usually ended up washing hundreds of dishes. I thank God that my body was strong enough to endure these labors, though I persisted in a constant state of pain and exhaustion.

Something had to give. I was working harder than I ever had, under nearly intolerable conditions—and still, I hadn't received a single Egyptian pound. How could I endure this for two or three years? It occurred to me that the promise of a two-to-three year work period had been made in the same email in which Mrs. Rahim had promised me my own sleeping area, the same email that stated that I would be accepted as a family member. Both of these turned out to be lies. With my passport in their hands, how could I know that I would ever be released?

It seems amazing to me now, but at the time I tolerated this treatment in the hopes that I would be paid. Even as I suffered, I always believed that my health and my faith would sustain me. And so they did; but, as I was about to learn, it would take something more—something beyond me—in order to liberate my body and soul from this situation.

The reality of bondage came to me as a dark and dire revelation. It happened during a family excursion to the coastal city of Alexandria. The extended family gathered there in Mrs. Rahim's mother's summer home for a week-long holiday. I was in charge of the three unruly children, Mrs. Rahim's daughter and her two male cousins. Knowing that the children could be bratty and ill-tempered, I prepared a number of activities.

On one particularly hot day, I found a garden hose and decided to turn the hose into a game. Picking it up, I announced, "Whoever gets hit by the water is out." I turned the stream toward the elder boy. He laughed and dodged it. Then I started laughing and chased him with the hose until he was soaked.

But not everyone was having a good time. Upset that she wasn't the center of attention, Mrs. Rahim's daughter had disappeared. She returned with her mother, who was livid.

"What have you done?" she said.

"Nothing," I replied. "We were just playing a game with the water hose."

But this provoked an angry tirade of curses. I quickly began to piece together that, based on the girl's testimony, she was accusing me of making inappropriate sexual comments to the kids and of touching them inappropriately. I was horrified by the accusations and even more horrified that the children themselves were behind the charges.

For nearly two hours, Mrs. Rahim and her mother berated me. They painted me as a degenerate and maniac. Mrs. Rahim's mother mockingly said that she could get me a man to sleep with, if that was the problem. Mrs. Rahim herself threatened to report me to the police. Without a passport and with a questionable work status, these threats terrified me. I tried to stand my ground and say that I was a Christian woman, that I would never do those horrible things. But my pleas only fueled their rage.

The fact that these accusations had come from the children was a disturbing sign. A feeling of terror and violation erupted inside me. All of the pain, rage, and humiliation I had endured since arriving in Egypt rose up in me.

For so many years, I had read Psalms 23—"The Lord is my shepherd, I shall not want"—without understanding it. As I read it through my tears in Alexandria, I realized I was now walking through the valley of the shadow of death. This much I knew: though in bondage to man, I served no one but God.

It took hundreds of years of slavery and oppression in this very land for God to reveal Himself to the Israelites. Just as the Israelites had gone to Egypt for economic reasons (a famine in their land), I too had sought relief from economic oppression in my homeland. Just as the Israelites were exploited as helpless foreigners, I was being abused for my labor. And just as the Israelites called out to God, so did I.

Realizing that I was in bondage was the first stage of my liberation—once I realized that my life was not merely difficult, but that I had been rendered helpless, I fully understood that all life is in the hands of the Creator.

As we returned to Cairo, the words of the prophet Hosea rang in my ears: "When [the Lord] roars, His children shall come fluttering out of the west. They shall flutter from Egypt like sparrows, from the land of Assyria like doves; and I will settle them in their homes, declares the Lord" (11:10–11). I viewed God's vow to save his children from Egypt and to return them home as His personal promise to me. And so, having prayed fervently four months earlier to find my way to Egypt, I now prayed even more fervently to end this nightmare, to return home and end my affliction.

Although strengthened with a newfound confidence, I kept a low profile, not knowing when or how I would be helped. Yet help came more quickly than even I had anticipated.

Although allotted only fifteen minutes of email contact a month, I found ways to increase my time a bit by sneaking over to a sympathetic neighbor's home. I had stayed in email contact with Ellen, the American woman for whom I had nearly worked. I took the same approach with Ellen that I had with my family and friends back in Kenya. I tried not to alarm them with details of my plight. I was afraid they would worry too much.

In an email to Ellen I wrote:

Everything here is fine apart from I check emails once a month for 15 mins and no going out except with the boss and no church for me as they are Muslims hence I work 24/7. All the same God is good all the time.

Haven't heard from you for a long time say hi to the entire family.

Please reply
SELINA

Ellen replied:

I am happy you found a job . . . how are things going? Tell me about the new family. What is it like over there? We are busy this summer doing wonderful things with the kids. Visiting friends, summer camp and staying busy working all day. it is quite stressful to be honest with you and some days i don't know how i get through . . . i look forward to hearing more from you and knowing more about your new life there. are your days as hectic as mine or worse? What exactly are you doing? Any cooking? I look forward to hearing back from you soon . . .

love . . . ellen

In my response to her email, I told Ellen how vexed I felt when they curbed my Internet access and forbade me from attending church. I detailed the harsh labor and the way Mrs. Rahim's daughter made up false accusations against me. I concluded the email by writing:

> Anyway I just hope all will go well with me; one thing I have learned is never get too annoyed as it will bring sickness to your bones and never say you're tired . . . [if you call me here] please don't let them know I emailed you as they haven't given me a chance to email this month. It will cause problems. You could say that my sister gave you this number as I haven't been responding to your emails.

Ellen replied:

> are they paying you? i just wanted to make sure that they are treating you with respect and not hurting you in any way. I saw a show on Oprah Winfrey about girls going to your area and being forced to work long hours with no pay . . . kind of like slavery. I hope they do not hurt you. Do you feel like you are safe and being cared for lovingly? If you fee[l] it is a disrespectful atmosphere for you please let me know and i will try to help you get [out] of there. Please be honest with me . . . thanks and send me the address . . .

These were the words I had been hoping to hear for many weeks. I hadn't wanted to trouble Ellen with my situation, but her email indicated to me that she was a perceptive and caring person. And when she said she wanted to help me, I knew she was serious.

I replied:

> I feel like a prisoner . . . really I need help to get out of here if it is possible to get to a better place. How can this

be done? They have my passport. They don't pay me, it's true (they send a small amount of money to my family when I ask them, but sometimes not). Now the boss is telling me to get off the computer . . .

Please write back and God bless you.
SAY HI TO THE FAMILY
SELINA.

The next few weeks were full of activity. I didn't know it at the time, but a volley of emails went back and forth from Ellen to the American Anti-Slavery Group (AASG) in Boston, who connected her with a Cairo-based human rights group called the Egyptian Initiative for Personal Rights (EIPR). Ellen and the leaders of AASG and EIPR formed a plan to help me escape. Although I didn't know the details of the plan, I knew something was happening. I got this email from Ellen:

I would like to speak with you by phone. Please set up a time when it is ok for you to speak and I also need the full address where you are living or the neighborhood you are living at . . . i am going to send my friend in cairo to meet with you as soon as possible wherever is best for you. . . . Ellen

With the help of the cook, who let me break the rules and use the Internet beyond my allotted time, I sent this reply:

Thanks for your mail. It has come in when I needed you most. I just complained that I was tired and needed to rest for 2 hours and the lady's mother and the lady said they can do anything to me, including taking me to the police. Please help me.

The next few days were marked by sneaking around, trying to read and send emails when the madam left the house for a moment. Although the cook was nervous about getting in trouble with the madam, she let me use her phone to receive calls. This became logistically difficult and a different tactic was needed.

A Cairo-based representative of the EIPR group called the Rahims a number of times. I was able to speak with him once, but that was it. Later I learned that he had called again to speak with me, but wasn't permitted. Soon things became even more complicated. Ellen and the human rights groups had contacted Mrs. Rahim's husband and threatened to take legal action.

This was a very dangerous time for me. My intentions to leave were now known, but I was still in the custody of the family. They could still do with me as they pleased. Mrs. Rahim tightened her hold on me. She tried to break my will. Although I didn't think it possible, she increased my workload, forcing me to scrub and polish everything repeatedly, until it shined. Mrs. Rahim also took new, stricter measures: I was no longer permitted to enter rooms that had any access—phone or Internet—to the outside world.

She re-issued the old threats: if I broke any of the rules or talked to anyone outside, she reserved the right to call the authorities. My back ached and I was depressed. Fear seized my heart: what if the family decided to relocate me somewhere else? I might never be discovered. I didn't know how far Mrs. Rahim was willing to go and this terrified me. Thoughts of freedom seemed remote indeed. But I didn't break.

I persisted in a state of limbo for weeks, hoping that the wheels were still turning on the outside. The phone would ring and the madam would pick it up and hang up. The madam and the cook would retreat into the kitchen and whisper nervously. The behavior of every member of the household grew more tense, more guarded—except, of course, the child, who remained as bratty as ever.

After a while I began to detect a change in the madam's behavior toward me. She seemed to be more detached than usual. Although still capable of abusive outbursts, she appeared to take little notice or interest in me. This seemed like a positive sign to me—my intuition said she was distancing herself from me before actually setting me free.

I was right: the human rights workers in Cairo and the United States had been persistent. Their message to the Rahims had apparently sunk in. In one chaotic hour I was told to pack my bags, call my friends for money, and prepare to fly home. I had to scrape the money for my departure together from the same sources that had lent me money to fly to Egypt (with some additional help from the human rights group). During my entire time with the Rahims, I never received any direct compensation.

It was strange to see how everyone acted once my sudden departure had been announced. The madam's husband was angry. He came to me and said, "Why didn't you tell me something was wrong?"

I thought, "If he doesn't know about his wife's behavior, he won't get it even if I tell him." The child, who for months had taunted and demeaned me, now cried inconsolably. She kept on repeating, "I don't want her to go, I don't want her to go." I found her behavior somewhat puzzling. On one hand, it was revealing that she didn't address this comment to me, but rather to her mother. I wasn't a real person to her, I was a plaything that her mother had brought home for her amusement. On the other hand, perhaps she had, in her childish way, forged some sort of twisted attachment to me.

As my plane home to Kenya took off from Cairo's airport, I thought about the child. She was born innocent and yet, at so young an age, was already mired in the mindset of her parents. I pitied her. As the plane cruised through the darkness I remembered my first flight in an airplane, over four months earlier. I recalled looking down on the works of man as they became smaller and smaller, thinking that God is remarkable for caring about this small world of ours.

As my plane, in the words of the prophet Hosea, "fluttered from Egypt like a sparrow," I looked out the window, into the darkness, and praised God for His goodness to me. I prayed for all of God's children, who made their homes on the earth below me. Then I fell into a deep and restful sleep.

Even though I have returned to my land, the experience of being a stranger in a foreign land will stay with me always. The Bible reminds the Israelites, even many years after they were delivered from bondage in Egypt, never to forget that once they were slaves. I understand this commandment to remember—not just my own story, but all those who remain in bondage.

Today Juma has rejoined her family but continues to seek employment as an au pair. Though her story carries ancient biblical cadences, it was modern communications technology that played a pivotal role in her enslavement and rescue. The vigilance of her friend Ellen, an American who only happened to learn about slavery in passing by watching Oprah Winfrey's TV show, is a reminder that being alert in your community can also help make a difference in the lives of people halfway around the world.

Chapter Seven

ATOP THE SECOND WAVE

TESTIMONY FROM A BELARUS PRISON

Sveta

The narrative below was collected from a young woman in prison. Why the young woman, named Sveta, ended up in jail does not become clear until the final few paragraphs. But what immediately emerges from this chapter's halting language and impressionistic style is the deep psychological scars of sex trafficking.

Sveta's testimony unfolds in a collage of incidents. We see her playing in kindergarten with her stuffed animals. We watch her helplessly surrounded by a group of boys intent on rape. And we follow her to the "Point" in downtown Moscow, where pimps peddle their girls to potential customers.

Sveta appears scarred, numb, and detached. She confessed her story to a social worker from a nongovernmental organization (NGO) that works closely with the International Organization for Migration (IOM). It was later edited into a narrative by a writer in America. Her story reveals how young women have become a lucrative though disposable commodity for sex-trafficking rings. And her frank description of the dehumanizing experience in part explains how she came to invert the roles of sex slave and pimp—how she came to ride atop the "second wave."

Time spent in prison fuses into one solid gray ribbon. It might be because your thoughts are constantly spinning around one and the same theme. Your daytime reflections find their way into your night dreams. Later, you can no longer distinguish between what you dreamt and what you were pondering during the night.

I grew up as an inquisitive and cheerful girl. That was what my kindergarten teacher used to tell my stepfather when he picked me up from school. I never knew or saw my biological father. My stepfather was kind to me and often bought something sweet for me on the way home.

Until I was about ten, my favorite pastime was sewing stuffed animals. My mom bought me special kits at a store, and I would neatly sew the pieces together and attach bright buttons to make them look like funny eyes. When I was in kindergarten, I wasn't able to fall asleep without my favorite toys, and I would even take them to school and put them right next to me in my little cot during nap time. They knew all my confessions and secret thoughts.

My mother explains to the investigator that her daughter grew withdrawn, silent, aloof. "She spent more time with her friends on the street. When she was only eleven, she left home for the first time. She didn't return for a few days. It all happened soon after that."

I didn't know those boys. I saw them occasionally in the streets of the town, but I never talked to them. They were much older and never noticed me and my friends. So I was surprised that day, when they stopped and asked my name. They started a conversation very quickly, and soon I was invited to the gym—"a place where you could sit and relax," they told me. My mother had never warned me not to go with the older boys. What could happen to me, I thought as I excitedly followed the laughing boys.

I still remember it vividly. I begged and cried and tried to break away from those six muscular bastards, who easily dominated me. They punched my face and stomach violently, tore my clothes to pieces. An eleven-year-old child couldn't withstand such humiliation and anguish. I fell unconscious while being raped, weakened from the fight.

It was two weeks of the same nightmare. By the time I saw my mother at last, I was empty and indifferent, staring blankly at the wall. Nobody could ever know what was inside me, what humiliation I was forced to suffer, how deeply I was degraded, and how desperately I asked God for help.

Eventually, there was a trial, and the rapists were sentenced to prison for various terms. My family still believes the court was too compassionate. I didn't remember their faces and names; I couldn't help the court, and the rapists didn't testify against each other. Only two of them were convicted, and because they were under age, they were not given severe sentences.

My brother, who had just turned eighteen, made up his mind to "correct" the court's verdict. Together with my cousin, he bought a sawed-off shotgun and stole a car. They started to hunt down the remaining rapists who, by the court's verdict, hadn't been put behind bars. When the police started to pursue the stolen vehicle, my brother and cousin fired at them. As a result, they ended up on plank beds in prison for sixteen years for armed resistance to police officers. These sentences were much longer terms than those the rapists had been forced to serve.

When I was thirteen, I gave birth to a son. His father was a country boy who lived next door to my grandmother. I used to visit her often. The doctors warned that I might not be able to bear all the burden of the pregnancy and delivery. My mother insisted that I keep the baby. "How could you kill a living being, especially one that has your blood?" she told me. "There is enough bread and sun for everyone. We will be able to raise the baby."

Everything happened as she said, and my mother had to raise her grandson all by herself.

"When did you leave the village?" the investigator asks me.

I hear my mother answer. "The boy was not even six months old when my daughter disappeared again for a long time. Only after a month and a half of unsuccessful inquiries did we learn that Sveta had been in Moscow. She called home saying just a couple of words, 'I am in Moscow. I am doing OK.'"

I met him at a bus stop. A man of about thirty was watching my cousin Jenya and me while we waited for the bus. The man listened closely to our conversation and then he walked up to us and started up small talk, asking us questions like "What time is it?" and "Will bus twelve take me to Coach Park?"

He invited us to a café and we accepted. He treated us to a beer. He told us that he was from Moscow, and he was visiting some friends. We didn't have a clue that our new acquaintance had planned that meeting for a long time. The encounter seemed totally accidental.

Before he had met us, the man had already learned almost everything about Jenya and me. His girlfriend lived in my village, and she told him about our families, what we did, who our friends were, how much our parents made, and what our thoughts were about sex.

Yes, we were meeting with men. Yes, we would agree to spend a night with our new friend—the night he promised to make romantic and unforgettable.

"You are so sexy," he said as he held our hands under the table in the cheap café. "Girls like you are being bathed in gold in Moscow. Let's go and you won't regret it. You'll be able to live on your own, afford to get whatever you want, and you'll depend on no one. You will also throw away the stuff you're wearing now and dress like famous actresses. And believe it or not, while living the high life, you'll be earning money for your family," he kept repeating.

It seemed like the man was reading our minds. He promised exactly the kind of life in Moscow that we had been dreaming about—a big city, money, and considerate, gallant, and—most important—wealthy men. We would have adventures and unconditional freedom! Freedom from tedious school, drinking mothers, and boring life.

A few days later, we boarded the Brest-Moscow train for the better life we had been promised. We didn't need any documents as our new friend had bought the tickets using other people's passports.

When we got to Moscow everything turned out differently. Our dream crashed against the reality: we had to pay back our debt—the money paid for our tickets and accommodation, food, and clothes. The man threatened to put us in jail if we tried to escape. Every day we were taken to the "Point," pushed into the client's car, and taken to hell.

The Point, the meeting ground where we were dropped every day, was almost in the city center. About sixty prostitutes, watched vigilantly by a so-called Mommy, stood down in the subway station on almost twenty-four-hour duty (starting at noon and finishing between three and four in the morning). Each girl came at her own price, and a client would order the girl he could afford.

Jenya and I lived in an apartment on the outskirts of Moscow with one other girl from Belarus. It had been rented especially for us. However, our place of residence was changed from time to time when the landlord would show up and refuse to continue renting the apartment. Also, there was a constant threat of being caught by the police during one of their searches for "haunts of vice." The police occasionally arrested us and took us to a local police division, where they would keep us for a couple of days, until we were released. We were not let in on the secret of our sudden release, but there were rumors that our pimp had just bought us out.

Documents and money were not kept in the apartment. There could be some cash in our pockets for shopping or just for the sake of taking a stroll, but strolling was the last thing we could think about after a night's work. When we finally finished the night's work and traveled home—by taxi in the best case, or in the worst case by public transportation—we would dream of just crashing onto the bed and sleeping, sleeping, and sleeping! A few hours of sleep and the pimp would show up to take us again to the Point. We had to be fully ready by the time he arrived—dressed with all our makeup on.

By the age of fourteen, I had come across different kinds of clients. It was especially scary to run into stoned teenagers. These guys had no mercy. They usually had little money, and for them it was a matter of honor to have a prostitute who couldn't turn them down. Sometimes they would pick up a girl, pay the Mommy for servicing two men, take the girl to the place and reveal that there were actually five or eight, or even more guys. If their physiology failed them, they could rape with a bottle, a banana, or with whatever fell into their hands.

There was no way to refuse to go with a client. Nobody dared to do it. The girls would be beaten violently and given no money for food. A prostitute was "to have a ride" for as many times as had been purchased. Once I was forced to serve twenty-four clients in twenty-four hours. I never got the promised "hundred dollar bill from a client." The client directly paid the Mommy who kept track of all the "ridden away" girls. The Mommy later paid the pimp who had delivered the prostitutes to the Point. The pimp gave me and his other girls a hundred Russian rubles each (a bit more than three U.S. dollars) for every "ride away."

"Money likes order," he used to say. "This will be enough to buy food so far. The rest I will keep myself. Otherwise you will waste the money, because you are too young and you

169

don't know how to deal with it." From the money he took from the Mommy, he paid for the apartment he rented for us and bought us clothes.

It was considered an indication of the pimp's special favor when he took a girl for a night for himself or for his friends. Although such a girl was thought of as lucky, it would cost a pimp nothing to beat her mercilessly. Once, the pimp didn't like Jenya's tone of voice. He made her undress, took off his belt, and flogged her back with the buckle till she started to bleed. Deep and long ugly scars will stay on her back forever.

Some other girls working with me at the Point advised us to take drugs. "Everything will be much brighter," they said, "and you won't feel the pain." So we did.

I told my story to the NGO representative, who implemented the IOM program in our town in November 2003, when I came back home after having been away for six months. My mother had seen an article in the town paper about the IOM counter-trafficking program in Belarus, and she called them when I returned. At that time, I said almost nothing about my stay in Moscow and answered the questions in monosyllables. No feeling, no regrets were left. I was empty. I agreed to cooperate with IOM, though. Over time, I gradually told them more details of my life.

I was able to return home when I realized that I was pregnant again. My stomach was getting round. It was an obvious obstacle to continuing my "work," and the pimp insisted on an abortion, but I refused. My pimp let me go home, threatening that he would be ready to go to the ends of the earth to get me if I didn't find someone to substitute for me.

He said, "Getting pregnant is your own fault, but breeding bastards is not what I hired you for."

I got home when I was six months pregnant. Jenya had also managed to obtain leave at that time—her chronic acute asthma turned out to be a good excuse. She also had to find a substitute. Under the severe stipulation that we find substitutes and recruit new girls, Jenya and I were released home for a while.

Three months after coming home, I gave birth to a healthy girl.

"That's OK, we will raise her as well," mother said.

So a fifteen-year-old child became a mother of two.

It was hard for me to live with the family and fulfill motherhood responsibilities. My parents were expecting me to be responsible, which in fact they hadn't taught me to be. My relations with my stepfather reached their lowest ebb. When he was drunk, and quite often when he was sober, he would take every chance to reproach me for delivering these children who were completely dependent on him and my mother.

My mother started yelling at me even more often, and it didn't matter whether she was sober or not. The family was disastrously poor, my mother was also pregnant, and my stepfather was the only breadwinner. My brother kept calling from prison, asking us to bring him more food, cigarettes, and warm clothes.

I called my pimp in Moscow several times to remind him of his debt, the money earned by me and taken away by him to be kept. He would always promise to pay, never forgetting to remind me to find and transfer to Moscow some new girls as soon as possible. Gradually, I started to realize that the pimp had just used me. For him, the girls were a kind of commodity that he looked after as a zealous farmer watches over his cattle.

When the officer of Morals and Drugs Enforcement Department asked Jenya and me to submit a petition against the pimp, we agreed to do so. The pimp was caught red-handed when he came to my town to recruit the new girls that Jenya and I had found for him. The new girls "accidentally" happened to be the police officers. The pimp was sentenced to a two-year imprisonment in a maximum-security closed convict colony.

I was getting psychological and legal assistance during the case investigation and the trial. My kids were not left without help.

During the investigation period, Jenya and I started taking drugs again, which we had first tried in Moscow. Jenya took everything of value out of her house that her mother hadn't yet boozed away. Everything that we managed to get for the carpets and crystal, we spent on drugs. Jenya left for Moscow again without even waiting for the pimp's trial.

I had to withstand incredible psychological pressure from my parents and my children, who required a lot of patience, care, and love, and from the trafficker's wife, the police, and the litigation. They were pressing from all sides. The pimp's wife showed up from Moscow, and at first she started threatening Jenya and me, and then she offered us lots of money if we would refuse to sue her husband. My mother and stepfather were concerned about the children a lot. The atmosphere in the house was really nerve-wracking.

On top of that, some strangers kept calling us from Moscow—mostly men who wanted to talk to me and threatened me now and then. Once, there was a call from the "business partner" of the convicted pimp. He promised to give me the money I earned.

"Come back to Moscow. I will pass you the tickets via a train conductor," he said.

One day I made up my mind. "I'm fed up with it all! I just have to go, and I'll see what happens!" I thought. At that point I hadn't decided whether I would resume being a prostitute. "I will see. If I run into a decent pimp . . . I will be smarter this time, and I will not let anyone keep the money I earn!"

I was very familiar with the prices: I knew exactly how much a Mommy made, what a pimp's cut was, and how little a share of the money the prostitutes got. My new pimp must figure out straight away that the standard scenario would not work on me.

Sure enough, when I arrived in Moscow, I was picked up and carried away atop the second wave. I became a full-time sex trafficker.

I walked to the Point as soon as I arrived in Moscow. The first pimp who approached me was well-known and well-connected.

"You know you can't work for yourself," he started. "Everyone knows you can't survive without the protection of a good pimp."

"I'm not going to be one of your girls," I told him.

We talked for a while longer, and he offered to promote me to the next level, to be a full-time recruiter. In this new capacity, I came back home again, right before New Year's Eve. This time I was not alone. My "guest" was a young man who was introduced to my mom as a fiancé. He was a security guard who escorted the girls to the clients and back. It was he who suggested that we team up, that together we could recruit a lot more new girls for a "better life" in Moscow and earn easy money. We went out every day, to bus stops, bars, and street hangouts, talking to girls and promising them jewelry and new, fascinating lives as city girls.

A month later, after throwing some of my new clothes into a suitcase, we unexpectedly left for Moscow with a bunch of new girls.

The pimp and I rented an apartment in a safer suburb of Moscow. The girls from Belarus and some other girls I knew from the Point had agreed to work for me and my pimp and lived in the apartment. I was in charge of bringing the girls to the Point and delivering to the pimp the money the girls earned and had given to the Mommy. The pimp occasionally gave me a few rubles for spending money.

When the police raided the apartment, we would move the girls to other pimps' apartments. The raiders were always from the special sex-trafficking unit of the Moscow City police—the district militia officers left us alone; they knew about these kinds of apartments and the pimps paid them to shut up.

My pimp allowed me to call home occasionally, and I was even able to send some stuffed animals home for my kids. I promised my mother that I would come back home by spring.

I returned in the beginning of March. Once again, I was escorted by a man. My new "admirer" was definitely older than forty. My new partner and I wanted to settle down in my town more or less permanently. He was looking for a job and kept saying that he was going to buy a house in the country. We traveled to Moscow several times to finalize some business deals. My mother was in a panic. My new boyfriend was trying to turn me against my parents.

"He persuaded my daughter to leave our home," my mother cries to the investigator. "He controlled her life and directed her activities."

At the end of May, IOM assisted in finding two girls that my new boyfriend and I had invited to Moscow with promises of well-paid jobs and money. That's what led me to this prison. It was my mother who eventually helped the police and IOM find two of the girls I took to Russia to work as prostitutes; she had gone to IOM for help.

Currently I am in the investigative isolation ward, accused of recruiting people for "sexual exploitation."

"What do you plan to do if you are released?" the investigator asks me.

"Yesterday my boyfriend told me that he loves me and that he will wait for me to marry regardless of the sentence," I tell him.

"He beat her!" my mother cuts in. "The girls that IOM found told the social worker he would thrash her."

I don't look at my mother and repeat to the investigator that my boyfriend "had nothing to do with it."

The investigator asks, "Did you feel sorry for the girls? You knew well enough what would happen to them."

"Nobody was sorry for me either, when they were taking me out."

He asks me what made the young girls leave behind both home and family and go as chance directed them.

"Greed. Everyone wants money, fast and a lot."

Since providing her story for this piece, Sveta was recognized as a victim of trafficking and released from prison. She is now receiving "reintegration assistance" and vocational training. She lives with her mother and her children in her hometown in Belarus. IOM hopes she will ultimately find a decent job and will learn to be a caring mother.

Chapter Eight

AMAZING GRACE

A SLAVE OWNER'S
AWAKENING IN MAURITANIA

Abdel Nasser Ould Yessa

> I once was lost
>   But now am found
> Was blind
>   But now I see
>   —*Amazing Grace*

Legend has it that these words, among the most inspiring in American folk music, were written by a former slave trader as a renunciation of his past. Our final chapter presents the story of a man who experienced a similar transformation.

It may seem strange to include in an anthology of slave narratives the tale of a former slave owner. But as Abdel Nasser Ould Yessa's life testifies, there is more to eradicating slavery than displaying the suffering of its victims. It is important to recognize those rare, brave individuals who dedicate their lives to fighting injustices that their friends, families, and society take for granted. Moreover, understanding the social mechanics of human bondage from the master's point of view is critical to disassembling slavery.

Over 1,000 years ago, Arab raiders from Morocco journeyed south and invaded Mauritania, overpowering the indigenous Africans and forcibly converting them to Islam. Today, descendants of those raiders, including Yessa's family, still own descendants of those Africans. As Arabs make up just 30 percent of Mauritania's population, they rely on their repression of the black majority in order to dominate the country's social and political life. Mauritania thus bears the dishonor of hosting the world's last outpost of institutionalized chattel slavery, with slaves owned as inheritable property.

Yessa, who does not speak English, has provided extensive interviews on how he came to reject Mauritanian's ingrained system of slavery. The following chapter, composed from Yessa's testimony, begins in the late 1960s, by an oasis on the edge of the Sahara desert, where Yessa's clan—a large entourage of wealthy, aristocratic Bedouins—has set up camp. They are there to celebrate his circumcision—and to give him a most unusual gift . . .

When I turned seven, my parents gave me the present I'd always wanted: my best friend.

It was the day of my circumcision ceremony. I sat in the ritual tent opposite a man with a waist-length beard and a knife large enough to behead me. All around me, slaves and courtiers chanted celebratory songs and hammered drums, creating a thundercloud of anticipation as the man with the knife knelt before me and grinned.

Onyx eyes flashing, he raised the knife.

The room went silent.

And then the knife struck—

Suddenly I was a man, and the man with the knife was yelling, "What do you want? Choose your gift!"

I could have asked for a camel. But for me it was a fait accompli.

I ran my eyes over the crowd until I spotted him: a squirrely black shape huddled in the back of the tent. The courtiers pulled him out and brought him to me. We both knew that he was mine. All I had to do was ask.

"Yebawwa," I yelled. "Give me Yebawwa!"

In that instant I became that character reviled in the Western world, a character who has largely disappeared from the face of the earth—but who still exists among my family, throughout my country, and in other select and ignored corners of the planet.

I became a slave owner.

It might sound appalling, but as a young boy I considered ownership of another human being not only my right, but an obligation to the slave. After all, I saw slaves as stupid and helpless. What could they do besides serve? Set free, they would wander out into the desert and starve to death. We masters had to protect them from themselves and their animal natures. Owning slaves was as much a responsibility as it was a luxury, and the idea that I belonged to a wrongful society never occurred to me.

In Mauritania slavery is a fact of birth. Just as I am of the highest caste—the warriors—because my father is, a slave is a slave because of his lineage. Everyone accepts this state of affairs, including the slaves themselves, which is part of the reason we abolitionists face such a difficult task.

But how did a slave owner become an abolitionist? To explain, I must go back to the desert.

Visiting my tribe in 1969 required traveling across the Sahara for several days, first by car and then, when the paved roads ended, by camel. Our desert entourage looked more like a small city than a temporary encampment; we traveled in a group of 500 families plus legions of slaves. Most nomadic Mauritanian camps were a tenth the size of ours. But our leader, the *emir*, was of noble birth. An ancient man, he had many wives and hundreds of grandchildren, of which I was one (and not a particularly outstanding one).

In a camp as big as ours, all of Mauritania's seven castes—warriors, clergy, courtiers, artists and genealogists, artisans, liberated slaves, and slaves—were represented. The physical structure of a camp reflected its social order; there were different kinds of tents for different social classes, just as any city has its wealthy and poor neighborhoods.

As a member of the aristocracy, I grew up in tents made of fine, unbleached cotton, majestic homes that announced their residents' high status. Surrounding such a tent you would find coarser woolen tents belonging to members of the middle class, people who were neither warriors nor slaves. And around the periphery of those tents were the cramped, black tents of the poor. A family's importance was measured by the number of satellite tents pitched around it in fealty.

Dotted between the tents was a fourth kind of "home." Too shabby to be called tents, they were more like collections of sticks, like a picket fence decimated by a windstorm. Some of these sticks had scraps of fabric attached. Under the most ideal circumstances they might have provided a slight buffer from the wind. That was where the slaves slept.

I can picture our camp on a blazing day. The sand gleams with heat, and on the whole, the scene is quiet; it is noon, the time when everyone has retired to the shade for the Mauritanian version of siesta. Goats bleat; horses snort. All around the big white tents, campfires burn, warming kettles of tea or pans of couscous. The smells of incense and camel droppings waft through the air. From far away drifts the voice of a man reading the Quran.

The flap of one white tent billows open, and a man wearing a *dishdasha* (Arab tunic) exits, eating from a handful of hard green dates. He has a moustache and wears thick glasses on the end of his nose. His expression is stern, severe, intelligent.

He is my father.

He walks over to listen to the news on our camp's portable radio. He likes to know what's going on in the world; he takes an interest in politics. Will Khruschev's Russia conquer the planet? Or will it go to Lyndon Johnson and the Americans? What will happen next between the Arabs and the Israelis?

Unlike most of the people in our camp, my father has a university education. Trained in Tunisia and France as a lawyer, he will soon go to work for the government as the country's first attorney general of Mauritanian rather than French birth. For right now, though, he is just having a snack and catching up on the news. He disappears into another large, cloud-white tent, and the camp is again quiet.

The only people out in the heat are black. Their bodies are wiry, hard, and glistening as they carry loads of firewood and pails of water. Hollow-cheeked and sluggish, they cook and tend to animals, leaping up when their masters call their names.

To an outsider, they may appear uncomfortable. But they know no purpose in life other than to obey. They are often told—and they believe—that service in this life earns reward in the next. As the Mauritanian saying goes, "paradise is under the master's foot."

Slaves keep our camp functioning; performing all household chores, minding children, massaging the feet of their masters. They work twenty-four hours a day, seven days a week, with no time off except the day of their marriage—if they are lucky. At all times, they have to stay within earshot, to come running the instant their master beckons. The harshest rebuke a slaveowner can give is, "You made me yell."

When storms sweep across the Sahara, dumping buckets of rain across the sand, slaves stand outside in the searing cold, holding up our tent as it sags under the weight of the water. I laugh with my brothers and sisters at the chattering of the slaves' teeth, a sound we call "teeth music."

One specific memory that lingers in my mind is moving day. Packing up and traveling with thousands of people was an epic event. We children loved it, relishing the thought of a new landscape—and perhaps some new friends, if our tribe were to encounter another.

But for slaves, moving was brutal, a nightmare. In the Sahara we recognize only two seasons: dry and rainy. As a result, the labor of moving occurred under either pounding rain or a scorching sun. One moving day I can remember, it was so hot that the slaves were practically drinking their own sweat as they collapsed tents, loaded animals, and dragged our possessions on their backs.

All the while, my mother sat under a palm tree, looking bored as she picked her teeth with a piece of wood.

Then two skinny slaves struggled to hoist the camp matriarch onto her saddle, a majestic palanquin fastened to the hump of a camel. In our society, the most beautiful women are the fattest. Families fatten their daughters with camel's milk, and a girl moving around might be scolded to hold still, for fear of developing muscles.

And so, an important woman like the matriarch was big enough to be incapable of moving at all. The slaves screamed as they heaved her onto the camel, as if loading a car onto the back of a bicycle. Finally they got her on, but nearly collapsed from exhaustion.

When the time came to actually travel, however, the camel could not stand up under all the weight. The matriarch grew angry. Everyone gathered round to watch, and the slaves knew they would be chastised unless they came up with a solution.

Finally, one did: they lit a fire and put it beneath the camel's rear. Even then, the animal—despite the flames against its skin—took its time getting up.

Hours later, when the caravan finally stopped, I watched the same slaves help the matriarch dismount. As they removed the bejeweled saddle, I saw its underside dripping with blood; the matriarch's weight had caused the seat to rip through the camel's skin. Several onlookers boasted that the animal's broken back confirmed the matriarch's beauty.

This moment encapsulated the worst parts of my culture: inequality, excess, unnoticed cruelty. Yet all people cared about was how fat and pretty the mistress was.

Despite these horrors, the Mauritanian warrior caste believes that it treats its slaves well. A warrior sees his slaves as an instrument of his prestige. To say a man's slaves are going hungry is to imply that he is either poor or a cheapskate. And so if a master has more than enough for himself, his slaves live well.

The problem is when the master does *not* have enough, in which case the slave is the first to go without. Near the end of my childhood, in the 1970s, terrible droughts brought hard times to all inhabitants of Mauritania, forcing the end of full-time nomadism, a way of life cultivated for millennia. My tribe was among the last to move to the city.

As hard as this period was for us, though, it was far harder on the slaves: they starved. Even today, when most people in Mauritania live in cities, many slaves function as domestic servants and die of malnutrition before the age of six.

Mauritanian Arabs do not buy and sell slaves in markets. Our slavery is not the brutal raiding of villages that exists today in Sudan; we successfully completed our raids centuries ago. And we do not operate the plantation market system that once thrived in the Caribbean. A Mauritanian warrior takes no pride in abusing those he owns; to act with compassion is seen as a sign of strength.

On the other hand, unlike in Sudan—where, in theory, a slave can flee and regain his freedom—few Mauritanian slaves would ever think to do that. Our caste system is over a thousand years old and very rigid. Master and slave see their positions as part of life's natural order. Slaves are born to one family, and stay there.

Unless, of course, they are sent away. I remember, once, after an engineer visited our entourage and showed us how to build basins to collect rainwater, my grandfather sent the man a six-year-old girl as a thank you gift. To give a slave as a present was not uncommon. It was accepted as normal— even as it tore families apart.

And what child questions the social order? I didn't. In fact, in some ways I was jealous of my slaves. Because they were considered animals, they weren't subject to as many rules as I was. They did not, for example, have to rise every day before dawn for the first prayer—as I did.

They knew how to hunt. I didn't understand that they had developed these skills in lieu of any real education. I simply saw them trapping tortoises and wild birds, doing things that looked fun to a young boy.

Slaves also had total sexual freedom. My friends and I discovered sex around sixteen, but slaves knew about it at thirteen; they were encouraged to breed. On top of that, while aristocratic marriages were arranged for political and economic reasons, slaves could marry for love, without material interests involved. It sounds romantic until you consider that their marriages could be broken up at any time.

Another thing slaves could do that I could not: express joy. As a warrior, I was not supposed to show emotion. A warrior's parents won't even say "my son" because it sounds too soft. I was taught to be proud, to walk with my eyes to the horizon.

But slaves, like animals, could be as emotional as they wanted. Sometimes I would creep out of my tent to watch their nightly exultations. Bodies shimmering in a circle one hundred strong, they would dance around a campfire to the sound of drums, the one-string violin, and the flute. I would take a seat in front, alongside my cousins who had also snuck out to be there. Voices twined up into the immense, black sky: songs about the harshness of life, a sort of Saharan version of the blues.

As I got older, and my relationship with slaves became more directly exploitative, I could not bring myself to come watch. Some nights I would lie in my clean, white tent, listening to them from far away.

Like all aristocratic newborns, I spent my first forty days nursing from my mother. Mauritanian tradition holds that the milk is richest then, and that, through suckling, the moral heritage of a tribe is passed down.

Following that, I got handed off to a wet nurse. It must have been jarring for the infant me, having the source of my dinner spontaneously change color.

Miriam was one of our family's many slaves, and she nursed me alongside her son, Yebawwa. That made us "milk brothers," and it meant that we were connected from our infancy.

Yebawwa was lucky to have been born close to me. A wet nurse gets treated much better than the average slave; her masters don't overwork her, and they give her plenty of food. In Yebawwa's case, his mother ate so much that he actually got fat while nursing, a condition that he continued to enjoy throughout his childhood.

I say "enjoy" because it's almost unheard of for a slave to be fat. In Mauritanian culture, obesity equals luxury, privilege, and nobility. Most people expected that, once Yebawwa got older, he would turn sinewy and lean, like all other slaves.

Interestingly, though, he managed to stay fat. That he achieved this was a sign of his own laziness and my family's relatively easy treatment of our slaves. At a young age Yebawwa had decided not to live the typical life of a slave. Instead of spending the day working, he would park himself in our main tent and announce that he wasn't moving. People entering and exiting would kick him out of the way, but he kept coming back and plopping down among the pillows: thick-skinned, smiling, unperturbed.

"Here," he'd say, "there's milk. There's meat. You have music, interesting people, and the beautiful smell of incense. It's almost the gates of Paradise. And I prefer to be almost in Paradise."

Speeches like this amused the adults, and earned him the right to goof off. He was our court jester. At mealtimes, he would stand by the door of the tent and count the platters as other slaves brought them to us.

"One . . . two . . . three . . ." His eyes would widen. "You're *still* hungry? How can you eat this much without dying?" When nobody was looking, he'd snatch a bit of food, or corner a younger, smaller slave and rob him of lunch.

As my milk brother, he was like my best friend, although our relationship existed in the context of my superiority and his obedience. For his part, Yebawwa didn't question the system, as long as he could use it to his advantage.

"Can I have some?" he would ask, hovering over my breakfast of couscous with sugared milk.

"Go away, donkey-ears," I would say, shoving him.

The truth is, I liked him. He was extraordinarily funny, and funny-looking: like a little desert Buddha, round-faced with a huge stomach. He had a long, fleshy "outie," which he would stick out on my command. I'd pinch him on the belly-button, and he would laugh.

One of our favorite games was to play camel-and-rider. Yebawwa would kneel in the sand and allow me to climb on his back.

"Faster!" I would yell, tapping him on the head with a stick. "Faster!"

It might sound degrading, but to us it was normal. And sometimes—just sometimes—we became involved in our games deeply enough to forget some of the differences between us. Children can do that.

At other times I would order him to sing. Closing his eyes, he would begin to belt—very badly. He had a wretched voice, renowned for its awfulness by all my friends, each of whom had his own little slave. We warrior children had a running competition for who owned the most amusing slave. Most of the time, I came out on top.

"Yebawwa, dance!"

"Yebawwa, show off your stomach!"

"Burp, Yebawwa!"

He was a born showman.

In addition to being exceptional in these ways, Yebawwa was known for his expressive sleep-talk. One afternoon, while sitting in our big white tent, he nodded off and began mumbling his life story. "The Yessas are cruel!" he moaned. "They don't give me enough to eat . . . they don't give me nice clothes for festivals."

Later, when I told him about what he'd said, he denied it angrily. This was the way it would go: his subconscious would spout, and it would be up to him to save face. It was important for him to appear happy, because as much as he hated his position in life, he recognized that, for a slave, he had an easy life.

And stranger still, another part of him was filled with love for his masters. When I chose Yebawwa as my circumcision gift, he was proud. Before, he had been the slave of a family, but now he *belonged*—belonged to a single person. He was *Abdel Nasser's* slave. And since I was considered a person with a bright future, my importance made him important. In a sense, when I became a man, so did he.

Soon after my circumcision, the droughts became unbearable. The nomadic life I'd grown up with was ending. Although my family would return to the desert every year for vacation, our new home would be the capital city, Nouakchott. I was seven, ready to begin a new phase of my life. With this move came some drastic changes.

On my first day of school, my father, younger brother, and I met our chauffeur outside and piled into his car. I was slated to begin primary school, and my younger brother was bound for Nouakchott's first kindergarten.

Not everyone smiled on this arrangement. Tahfadhna, Yebawwa's older sister and for years our babysitter, complained bitterly. "Now what am I going to do?" she moaned.

Although she was nine—two years older than I—her life had been reduced to the task of taking care of my brother and me. Without us, her sense of purpose shriveled up. A slave's need for his master is one of the hardest things for Westerners to understand. This psychological dependency means that Mauritanians do not have to beat or chain their slaves; the slave simply cannot imagine a world in which he is free.

At the time, however, I did not think of this. I was concerned only about the terrifying prospect of a day away from home. From birth I had been surrounded by family: uncles, aunts, cousins to fill a battalion, and for every relative a retinue of slaves. Now I was alone, an undistinguished student among peers.

This was precisely the point. I could have studied anywhere, but as a servant of the state, my father decided that I had to go to public school with everyone else.

"Everyone else" consisted of Arabs and Negro-Africans (free blacks), French-speaking and Arabic-speaking, all crammed in one room. This environment was more democratic than what I'd grown up with, but it was far from complete integration. To begin with, boys outnumbered girls two to one. Furthermore, there were no European children; they attended their own *lycée*. And obviously, there were no slaves.

Not in the classroom, at least. If you looked harder, you could see slaves everywhere. The woman who sold *bonbons* outside the school was a slave. The school guard was a slave. The janitorial staff consisted entirely of slaves. In school, as in all areas of Mauritanian society, the fuel of slave labor made everything possible.

My father spent his life establishing firm principles and then negotiating down from them. For example, despite his insistence that I go to school with the common folk, he was dismayed when my academic performance was at their level. Actually, it was worse than that; compared to other upper-class children, my performance was near the bottom.

A short investigation turned up the reason. All the other rich children—sons and daughters of high-ranking functionaries—had private tutors.

So my father temporarily set aside his principles of equality and civil service, and got me a tutor, too.

Monsieur Tomas was the city's most popular and well-regarded European tutor. He arrived at our house disheveled, unshaven, with a huge red nose like a siren. His nails were unclipped, and he spoke as though he had a mouth full of gum. Looking back, I realize that he was probably the closest thing to a hippie ever to set foot in Mauritania.

What characterized him most was a detachment from materialism. He maintained a long, elaborate theory about Western culture that had compelled him to wander from Belgium to North Africa: "Everything in the West is necrotic. Your life's over as soon as it begins. You're programmed for studies, work, a house, a car. You save up for retirement. Your kids grow up, they come to visit you—rarely. Then they put you in the old age home." He would raise one long-nailed finger. "And I refuse to end like that."

We had private lessons; or else he would gather a group of us at one student's home, and there begin his idiosyncratic form of education.

"I'm cultivating the Byronic spirit," he would say, declaiming Romantic poetry. "Hence, I am melancholy." Other favorites of his included Rimbaud and the French bohemian poet Gerard de Nerval ("Crazy," he said, "but *the best*"). With one fist raised, he shouted and recited. Afterward he'd be physically exhausted, mopping his brow with his sleeve, cursing under his breath and then instantly apologizing.

"*Whore!* Oh—excuse me, excuse me . . ."

Sometimes he assembled impromptu theatrical pieces, mostly vaudevilles and salon comedies by Marivaux. It must have looked absurd: a gaggle of twelve-year-old Arab boys engaged in banter from the 1830s. But we had fun—except for those playing female roles; M. Tomas could not convince us that this was an admirable thing for a boy to do.

Most of the time, he drilled me on my French. He brought me Victor Hugo and the fables of Jean de la Fontaine. To improve my penmanship, he gave dictations, standing over my shoulder as I scrawled out Latin characters.

"Monsieur Ould Yessa," he would say, "you write . . . like a *fly shitting*. Oh—excuse me, excuse me . . ."

Oddly, this ragged, swearing man had the utmost sense of decorum when it came to diction, table manners, and etiquette.

One time he showed up at my house with a sack of candles, crystal, silverware, and plates. He'd gone around to every European in Nouakchott, borrowing goods.

"Today," he said, pinning up a pair of loaned drapes, "we're going to learn the art of the table: *savoir vivre!*"

He tossed out a tablecloth and laid two settings, as though we were expecting a head of state. "Now close your eyes," he said, lighting the candles, "and pretend you're in Versailles."

He then gave an elaborate lesson on how to behave at a dinner party. One thanked the hostess, not the host. One never brought flowers; one sent them the next day, with a note. One never brought food. Bringing alcohol was the ultimate vulgarism. Hands visible at all times. Fork to the mouth, not mouth to the fork. Napkin in lap. Wipe the mouth before and after drinking. Never serve oneself; never take seconds unless offered. A trip to the restroom required invoking the formula: *Madame, I ask of you permission to ex-*

cuse myself. Say nothing of the food. And don't speak about money, religion, or politics, either. At the end of the meal, if one wanted to compliment the hostess, one said, "Madame, it was *exquisite.*"

Not "good." Not "great."

Exquisite.

It took me a long time to realize that the manners he taught were hopelessly out of date. Years later, when I was adjusting to life in Paris, all his archaic rules would pop into my head, dictating my comportment. People would invite me for a meal, and I'd send flowers the next day—with a note. Women had no idea what to make of me, but they were always *très charmés.* It was all thanks to M. Tomas's manners.

His own personal conduct? Another story.

"Son of a bitch! Oh—excuse me, excuse me . . ."

He was at once wildly progressive and staunchly old-fashioned; derisive of his background, yet firm that I should appreciate European culture. Whenever he spied someone who had an air of importance but lacked real power, he said, "Oh, look: there goes the king of Belgium."

When I turned fifteen, M. Tomas began teaching me about the French Revolution. He started with a review of the great movements, a history of ideas. None of it touched me deeply, because he presented the information in an academic manner. From the beginning, though, he must have identified some democratic spirit in me, because he constantly urged me to go to the local French Cultural Center.

"Your son is bored," he told my parents. "He comes home from school, and what does he do? He sits. He's understimulated. It isn't fit for a child like him."

My parents agreed. They didn't want me resorting to what most Mauritanian boys my age did for fun: hanging out in the streets.

For my part, I was fascinated by poor kids, the ones who washed windshields and begged for money. They sold contraband cigarettes and hung out by the cinemas, waiting for enough change to go in and catch a kung fu movie or an American western. They played with old tires, and salvaged bits of trash to build ingenious toy airplanes.

The only time I had friends of this sort was in the beginning of my school days. Back then, few houses in Mauritania had electricity. Students worked by the light of streetlamps, or else not at all. I got permission for two of my classmates to come over and use our indoor lights to do their homework. At one point, we went out to the backyard for a break, and they began demonstrating the moves they'd picked up watching kung fu. I thought it was great, but my parents forbade them from coming back in the house.

"They can use the lights of our courtyard," my mother said, "but that's all."

My friends found a new place to work.

By age twelve, the only contact I had with street kids came when we pulled up at an intersection. A dapper policeman would halt us with a raised hand; Nouakchott still had no traffic signals. As I lowered the windows, a throng would gather round to admire our Peugot. "Man, take a look at this . . ."

The chauffeur would edge the car forward. "Get lost, bandits!"

"Up yours!" they'd shout.

As the driver pulled away, I would turn back to look. It amazed me how quick these children were with a retort. With their strained faces and broken voices, they seemed prematurely old. They appealed to my restless spirit; I wanted to be with them.

But I was not allowed. So I was bored.

"Look at him!" M. Tomas said. "He's losing his mind. And, practically next door, there's a library full of books that he would be happy to get his hands on."

My father nodded. "You should go over and have a look."

I thought, *more* school?

The French Cultural Center (FCC) sits inside the embassy, at the western edge of the city, near the ocean. The building is so big that Mauritanians joke that it hasn't yet been liberated, that it's still colonized. Every afternoon the smell of the sea wafts as far as its gates—and stops there, as though Europeans have a monopoly on pleasant sensations.

To me, age twelve, it seemed like a building full of well-behaved children accompanying their dour parents. It lacked any trace of joy. I wanted to be normal, and as far as I could tell, normal Arab kids didn't hang out after school reading books in French. "No thanks," I told my parents. At that point they resorted to force, instructing the chauffeur to bring me there after school.

The first time I arrived, the driver walked me inside. We passed through the gates and into a sprawling, symmetrical garden with a gorgeous aroma. The flowers and the natty people walking about pleased me, but simultaneously stirred up disagreeable memories of a hospital. In both places you felt the same sense of rectitude, the same need to keep things proper at all costs. It scared me.

At the front desk we met a fifty-year-old woman with a masculine face and the voice of a horse. "Yes?" she demanded.

My parents had called in advance, so the chauffeur gave my name.

"Aha, Monsieur Ould Yessa." She launched into a lengthy recitation of the house rules, concluding with a stiff flourish, "Follow me."

The three of us started down the hall. Artwork covered the walls. The center had a darkroom, and many of the photos on display had been taken by French travelers passing through the desert.

"And here are the reading rooms . . ." The woman turned sharply and studied me. "How old are you?" Before I could answer, she said, "No matter. Come along."

The FCC functioned mainly as a library, with three floors of books that got more sophisticated as you went higher up. The lady led me straight to the children's reading room.

"You'll start here," she said.

The chauffeur must have sensed my apprehension. "I'm going to wait outside," he said, "but if you want to leave, come find me, and we'll go home."

Left to fend for myself, I browsed shelves filled with cartoon books. The other kids watched me. One by one, they started to come up to me, offering opinions and pressing their favorites on me.

"This *Asterix and Obelix* is the best!" one said.

"No, that's rubbish, read this one . . ."

"*This!*" Somebody shoved a copy of *Tintin in the Land of Black Gold* into my hands.

Without anything else to do, I opened it up. It told the story of a Belgian reporter coming to Arabian lands to solve a mystery involving exploding petroleum pipelines. It was close enough to home to pique my interest, and I sequestered myself in a corner. As soon as I'd finished it, I picked up another cartoon book and dove into that. I read with such fervor that I didn't look up until someone knocked on the door and announced, "We're closing! Clear the room, please!"

I ran back into the hallway clutching several books.

"I'd like to check these out, please," I told the lady at the front desk.

She sneered at me. "You cannot."

"Why?"

"Your card has not yet been signed by the director. Put them back."

I was furious. As soon as I had gotten into the idling car, I began making plans to get back to the center as soon as possible.

The thought stayed with me all night. All I could think about was that stupendous library and my burning desire to read. The next day I trudged through my classes, and when the chauffeur came to fetch me I told him, "Not home! Straight to the center!"

I was captivated by the FCC's curious ambiance, the tension between control and freedom. The moment I entered the building, I became subject to a barrelful of rules. I couldn't wander around; I had to observe the guidelines for taking out and taking care of books; I had to keep my voice down.

At the same time, I had complete intellectual license. Nobody told me what to look at. Nobody discouraged me from thinking, or tried to shape my impressions of what I read. Nobody cared if I consumed cartoon book after cartoon book.

In a matter of months I had torn through the entire children's section. A new world had been created beneath my feet, and its geography taught strange lessons.

Tintin didn't own slaves. Neither did Lucky Luke. In fact, *nobody* in the stories owned a slave. It was very odd; the reality that I knew did not map to the reality of these characters. I remembered something M. Tomas had once mentioned: that some societies didn't use slaves. I'd found this concept too difficult to comprehend, and had filed it in the same obscure mental cabinet where I put most of his bizarre ideas.

But now I was staring at the evidence. These characters—characters I spent my free time with, characters that I loved—didn't live like I did.

Finally, one day while reading *Asterix and Obelix* (a comic book set in ancient Rome), I came across pictures of slaves being thrown to the lions at the Coliseum.

Aha!, I thought. Here's where they've been hiding them.

Reviewing the story, however, I noticed several differences between the cartoon version of slavery and the slavery I knew. The slaves were white. They were well-fed. They laughed, and they looked happy. Of course, I was reading a comic book, with sanitized imagery. Nevertheless, I could tell that whoever had written this story didn't know the first thing about real slavery.

My surprise was the surprise of a child, not moral indignation so much as confusion. I finished the book and put it back on the shelf, like the lady at the front desk had instructed me to do. When I went home, I didn't ask my parents about the things I'd discovered. My thoughts and questions stayed bottled in my head, where they began a slow, inexorable churning. The scales had not tipped, but they had begun to wobble.

Running the gamut of the children's reading room entitled me to move to the second floor of the library. I ascended a long, creaky wooden staircase, the first one I'd ever seen. Every time it shrieked, I feared it would collapse.

The second floor housed an extensive collection of literature, both young adult and general. There I spent a good part of my youth. I completed Agatha Christie and John Le Carré. As I read and read, my tastes grew more advanced. I moved on to Russian literature and the French classics. I did not realize it, but I was becoming an aesthete.

It was not until age fifteen that I dared to venture to the library's third floor, a place whose very name rang of obscure and distant writings: philosophy, ethics, history. I was through with stories. I wanted to read about ideas, and to do that I had to take yet another trip up the creaky wooden staircase.

On the first floor, a reader had to contend with street noise and foot traffic from the foyer. On the second floor he had to close his ears to block out the clomp of shoes treading above.

On the third floor, silence reigned. It felt holy.

The demographics changed, as well: adults—and only a handful. Though the room was attractively laid out, it did not seem particularly popular. Apparently, most people didn't care to read about ideas.

One glance at the shelves sufficed to intimidate me. I tiptoed around, sweating lightly, until I found the section on politics. I thumbed the colorful spines until I found a book more majestic and magisterial than the rest. Its smooth vellum cover bore the title *The Anthology of French Constitutions*. I opened it up and began to read.

"Article 1. Men are born and remain free and equal in rights."

What?

I thought perhaps I'd misunderstood it, so I read it again.

"Men are born and remain free and equal in rights. Social distinctions may be founded only upon the general good."

It was the most interesting sentence I'd ever read in my life.

The next one wasn't so bad, either.

"Article 2. The aim of all political association is the preservation of the natural and imprescriptible rights of man. These rights are liberty, property, security, and resistance to oppression."

My vocabulary contained all of these words. Yet I had never conceived of them being put together in this way. It was like seeing your clothes on another person.

Unable to sit down, I flipped back to the first article and read again.

Men are born and remain free and equal in rights.

Men are born and remain free and equal.

Men are free and equal.

Men are free—

"Closing! We're closing!"

People gathered their belongings and headed down the creaky stairs, but I kept reading until the guards came to throw me out. Clasping the book under my arm, I hurried to check it out.

"This title is not part of the borrowing library," the librarian told me. "It is for in-house consultation only." She pointed me back upstairs.

I returned to the third floor, slid the book back into place, and staggered out of the center as though I had been kicked in the gut.

Men are born and remain free and equal in rights.

Maybe it didn't say that, I thought. Maybe it said men are *not* born free and equal. Maybe I was too tired to read it correctly.

But I did read it correctly. I read it enough times to remember the way the print looked on the page.

Men are born and remain free and equal in rights.

Intoxicating, highly subversive, this sentence was, I decided, either completely false or completely true. If it was false then everything was fine. My family, my past, my country, my ideas of right and wrong: they all retained their moral authority.

But if it was true—

Men are born and remain free and equal in rights.

If it was true, then my entire life was a lie.

Over the next few years I underwent a profound transformation. I read *The Diary of Anne Frank* huddled in my bed at night, trembling with fear for the young girl who might be caught. Her diary led me to the larger literature of the Shoah—the testimony of Holocaust survivors—and then to writings of Soviet dissidents. Their stories of nonviolent dissent and dignity in the face of oppression moved me greatly.

My self-education led me to understand how far behind my culture was: advances in civil rights that had taken place in eighteenth-century Europe still had not reached us. It humiliated me; my adolescent spirit rebelled. By age sixteen I had become fully converted to the cause of freedom. I began to put up posters in my room—Gandhi, Martin Luther King, and the Sudanese reformer Mahmoud Muhammad Taha (who was hanged in Khartoum for standing up for individual liberty)—all of whom appealed to my teenage sense of drama.

That summer, when my family returned to the desert for our annual three months of nomadism, I tried to make my case to members of my family. I told my aunt Neha that I had decided to become an abolitionist.

She exploded with laughter. "Your father, when he went to study abroad, came home saying the same things. A real revolutionary, he was. He wouldn't let slaves milk cows for him; he wanted to do it himself. Everyone came to watch him act out this scandal. You should have seen it, then you'd understand: hair in the pail, the cow pissing in the bucket. Even the slaves laughed at him. He turned to them and said, 'Don't mock me, I'm doing this for you.' And right then, the cow kicked him over." She snorted. "After that, things returned to their natural order. So go ahead, do what you want."

I refused to listen, of course. I marched out to the fields, where the slaves were harvesting grain. With great force, I began lecturing them about equality and liberty, the French Revolution, the open land movement, the emancipation of black slaves in America. They nodded and smiled. "Mmhmmm, how interesting . . ."

I saw that I was being ignored, so I went instead to gather a few friends, fellow Arabs sympathetic to my new ideas. We spent hours debating what I'd read and imagining what Mauritania might look like with slavery abolished. And while we speechified, our slaves waited on us, bringing us tea or water to wash our hands. Only in retrospect have I come to perceive the absurdity of this scene. We were so obsessed with our big ideas that we failed to notice the necks beneath our feet.

I then went to find Yebawwa, whom I hadn't seen in almost a year. He didn't come with me when my family went to the city, because although I was his owner in name, in reality he belonged (and still belongs) to several people. My aunt Neha—the same one who'd laughed at me—owns 50 percent of him, and her children own the rest. If I die, my stake in him reverts to my cousins.

When I found him, he leapt up, overjoyed to see me. And relieved: his craftiness always earned him a fair number of enemies among the other slaves, and without me around, he lacked any sort of authority. He asked me how I liked the city and prodded me for the gift I always brought when we returned to the desert.

Like my aunt, he found the idea of me becoming an abolitionist hilarious. "My master's funny," he said. "I was born to be a slave, and I'll always be a slave. If my master doesn't want me, I must've done something wrong."

I tried to talk to him in the simplest terms. "We," I said, "*we* are the slaves. Not you. We can't do anything with our own hands. *You* have power. *You* built this country. All you are missing is confidence."

He scratched his head and chuckled. "We are lazy. We think with our stomachs. We're here to serve; that's what God wants. My master was created for poetry, for beautiful things. He is fine and strong. We are unfinished. God forgot to refine us; he was too busy to finish us."

He pointed across the camp, to a slave bent under a basket of laundry. "Look at that slave. He walks like a duck. He can be a free man? Look at him!" He laughed and shook his head. Then he looked at me with pity, as though I had failed to grasp something obvious, something any child can understand. As though I refused to believe in gravity.

What I refused to accept, though, was the worldview that had been fed to both Yebawwa and me throughout our childhoods. As an emerging human rights activist, I was determined to find a way to break through.

Yet the mental chains of slavery afflict both slave and master. My first trip to France as a young adult to study at the university in Bordeaux was a mild tragedy. I had to carry my own suitcase. I had no idea how to wash my own socks, so I simply threw dirty ones away and bought new ones to replace them. When the school cafeteria closed for a long weekend, I suffered for two days without eating. I had never cooked for myself in my entire life. Finally I broke down and bought some eggs, crushed them in a pan and cooked them—shell and all.

To adjust to life without slavery, I had a long learning experience ahead of me. I would have to learn how to live like an independent human being—and how to use my freedom to help liberate the thousands my own society had marked for slavery. But I was ready for the challenge, eager to lose the identity of "slave owner" and accept a new identity as "abolitionist."

In 1995, against his family's wishes, Yessa co-founded the anti-slavery group S.O.S. Slaves Mauritania, along with several former slaves (see http://www.iAbolish.org/sos). After he gave an interview to Radio France, the Mauritanian government issued an arrest warrant for him on grounds of "defaming the state." He then spent ten years exiled in Paris, serving as S.O.S. Slaves' foreign secretary and working tirelessly to build international pressure on the Mauritanian regime.

His story demonstrates that all it takes is one book, one chapter—one sentence—to inspire personal transformation. Maybe it can inspire you, too. Turn to the epilogue that follows for a guide on how you can get active and help stop slavery around world.

WHERE YOU COME IN

Jesse Sage and Liora Kasten

For some readers, the journey ends here. Eight individuals from around the world have shared the gritty, intimate details of their encounters with modern day slavery. But now it seems time to put the book down and move on.

Yet, we hope that you will tarry a moment longer to consider two nagging questions: "Why does the world still allow human bondage?" and "What can I do to help eradicate it?" Neither question has a simple answer. But to grapple with both questions is to cut to the heart of the problem underlying the narratives you have just read.

THE GREAT FAILURE

Why did the hospital staff not recognize that Jill Leighton was being held as a forced prostitute? How could the Lebanese job placement agency have abandoned Beatrice Fernando to domestic slavery? Why didn't the international media cover the slave raid on Abuk Bak's village? How could millions of Mauritanians (not to mention hundreds of European expatriates in Mauritania) accept slavery as an everyday social institution?

Although there are no satisfying moral explanations, several key factors have enabled slavery to thrive into the twenty-first century. First, human trafficking is, in a way, the "perfect crime." Slaveholders take advantage of vulnerable individuals who often find themselves in a strange new land where they cannot communicate. The costs of this illicit trade are low and the profit margins, as Sveta herself discovered, can be quite high.

Many victims are easily entrapped because they are unaware of the prevalence of slavery in contemporary society. Slaveholders prey on individuals so eager for work that they are ready to take risks—individuals who do not understand the warning signs until it is too late. Then, like Selina, they find themselves in strange countries, stripped of their passports, and afraid of the police, who might come to arrest them.

At the same time, the general public does not realize that slavery still exists and, therefore, does little or nothing to intervene. Even if they have heard occasional news reports about "human trafficking," most individuals rarely imagine it could happen in their own neighborhood. As a result, Micheline Slattery can be held in suburban settings, take public transportation, and even attend the local high school without arousing suspicion of her enslavement.

Beyond the organized crime trafficking syndicates and individual slaveholders, human bondage continues to be employed by certain dictatorial regimes as a means of social control. Burma, China, North Korea, and Sudan are some of the more prominent examples of governments who direct forced labor campaigns (as testified to by Harry Wu). The dictators at the helm do not openly declare a pro-slavery policy, but nonetheless engage in ruthless internal slavery campaigns. They rely on the corrupt politics of the United Nations Human Rights Commission—where many of them hold prominent positions—to prevent any substantial international censure.

THE HUMAN RIGHTS COMPLEX

Dictators are unwittingly aided by the international media's and the human rights community's lack of clear priorities. If the slave raiders who abducted Abuk Bak and brought her to a slave pen were from Denmark, leading journalists and the human rights establishment would have raised a major cry. Instead, the raiders were sent by a radical Arab-Islamist regime—and the world largely yawned.

There are several factors for this failure to hold non-Western dictators and human rights violators accountable. One of the most provocative explanations has been formulated by Dr. Charles Jacobs, president and co-founder of the American Anti-Slavery Group, a veteran activist who struggled for years to get reporters and major human rights groups to pay attention to slavery in Sudan. Shocked by the largely indifferent response, Jacobs tried to understand why the human rights establishment devotes so much energy to certain atrocities but not to others.

Jacobs labels his theory of human rights selectivity the "human rights complex." The idea is that Western journalists and human rights activists, who are overwhelmingly middle-class and Caucasian, are particularly animated to protest against evils done by people like themselves. "Not in my name" is the banner slogan that captures the sentiments of those eager to show they are not like white racists or imperialists. Yet when evil is done by non-Westerners, many of these protestors hesitate, either because they feel they do not have a moral standing to condemn "others" or simply because their main interest is improving (or condemning) Western behavior.

If you want to know whether a human rights atrocity will get attention, Jacobs suggests, look at the identity of the oppressor, not the degree of the abuse or the identity of the oppressed. Apartheid by whites in South Africa mobilizes the human rights establishment. Enslavement of blacks by Arabs in North Africa does not. And so, abuses by Western governments attract intense scrutiny, while dictators and others who are "not like us" rarely face concerted campaigns. Inaction driven by misguided political correctness means that the human rights establishment is often unable to identify and counter abuses perpetrated by radical regimes.

It also bears noting that Western human rights activists are typically intellectuals and thus understandably relate most easily to prisoners of conscience: dissidents who suffer for their ideological beliefs. Slaves, however, are usually ordinary (sometimes even illiterate) individuals who do not suffer for an inspiring political stand. If they do not have the "luxury" of having a Western oppressor, they are all too often forgotten.

The "human rights complex" diagnosed by Jacobs is a challenge to all human rights advocates. Certainly there are notable exceptions to the theory, including important campaigns by inspiring grassroots activists. But both international media outlets and the human rights leadership are overdue for introspection on their reporting and campaigning priorities. For those enslaved around the world, the sooner this re-examination comes, the better.

The good news is that the world is waking up to the problem of contemporary slavery. (In part, the growing awareness came as cases of human bondage were identified in Europe and the United States.) One of the most significant breakthroughs came in 2000 when the U.S. Congress came together in a rare bi-partisan move to pass landmark anti-trafficking legislation. The law mandated that the State Department monitor slavery worldwide and produce an annual report ranking governments based on their performance in the struggle to eradicate slavery. The Justice Department simultaneously launched a toll-free trafficking hotline, special visas for trafficking victims, and an anti-trafficking taskforce.

Non-governmental organizations have also begun to step up to the challenge, implementing anti-trafficking programs in local communities and in countries around the world. Many of the survivors who work with us are now highly sought-after speakers to community groups and address thousands of Americans every year. In 1994, the founders of our organization lobbied Amnesty International to add slavery to its mandate—but failed when Amnesty's board stalled on the resolution; by 2005, Amnesty was proudly highlighting the countering of human trafficking as a central campaign.

We have come a long way, but we still have far to go.

BECOMING AN ABOLITIONIST

You can play a key role in advancing the struggle against slavery. You can help educate the public that slavery still exists, pressure leaders to take stronger action, and provide direct aid to rehabilitation programs. Here are a few ways to make an immediate impact:

Join the anti-slavery movement

After you finish this book, don't drop out. Stay connected by signing up for the American Anti-Slavery Group's online action network. Over 30,000 people receive our e-mail action alerts and together send letters and faxes to pressure international leaders. It takes only a minute of your time every month to participate in the Freedom Action Network's campaigns. Sign up today at www.iAbolish.org.

Invite a survivor speaker to your community

A better informed public can more easily identify local cases of human trafficking and pressure international leaders to act against slavery. But many Americans still do not know that slavery still exists. A great way to educate your community is to bring in survivor speakers. Several contributors to this anthology, as well as other survivors, regularly speak to schools, congregations, and civic groups. To learn more about inviting a survivor speaker, call toll-free 1–800–884–0719.

Educate others

The American Anti-Slavery Group has produced a free curriculum to teach students about contemporary slavery (see iAbolish.org), and several other human rights groups distribute free educational materials. If you are not a teacher, you can still recommend this book (and others on modern day slavery) to friends and relatives. Or simply direct them to the educational web portal www.iAbolish.org.

Don't be afraid to ask questions

Be a responsible consumer and make sure your purchases are not padding the pockets of traffickers. Also, be a vigilant citizen by staying on the look-out for trademark signs of people being held as slaves in your community. Ordinary citizens have become rescuers in many American cities and towns simply by being alert. Look for evidence that a person is being controlled, abused, has limited movement, exhibits fear or depression, and/or has no passport or identification. If you suspect a case, call the Trafficking Information and Referral Hotline at 1-888-373-7888.

Design your own campaign

Some of the best ideas come up from the grassroots level. Students—from 5th grade through college—have created outstanding campaigns to build awareness, raise money to support the anti-slavery movement, and pressure international leaders. Just because you are not an "expert" does not mean you cannot implement your own innovative campaign. The anti-slavery movement always needs fresh thinking from activists of all ages. For more information on how to get involved, visit www.iAbolish.org/activist.

THE NEXT GENERATION OF HARRIET TUBMANS

For Americans, addressing modern day slavery also means confronting our country's past. Although the enslavement of

African Americans was outlawed in 1865, we still grapple with its effects. One small way we can help heal the wounds of that system of chattel slavery is to stand up as abolitionists again today. All Americans—including descendents of slaves and slaveholders—can exercise their freedom to extend a hand to the millions now held in bondage around the world.

If the slave narratives in this collection have touched your heart and kindled a spark of activism inside you, then we encourage you to put down this book and join our movement to end slavery—once and for all.

By becoming an abolitionist you will be able to say, in the immortal words of escaped-slave-turned-abolitionist Harriet Tubman: "I have heard their groans and sighs, and seen their tears, and I would give every drop of blood in my veins to set them free."

CONTRIBUTORS

GLORIA STEINEM
Gloria Steinem has been called "America's most influential, eloquent, and revered feminist" and is the founder of *Ms.* magazine. A former assistant editor at *New York* magazine, she co-founded the National Women's Political Caucus and the Coalition of Labor Union Women. She is the author of *Outrageous Acts and Everyday Rebellions* and *Revolution from Within: A Book of Self-Esteem.*

LIORA KASTEN
Liora Kasten is the Program Director of the American Anti-Slavery Group. Her abolitionist work with survivors of slavery has brought her to India and Sudan, and she has collaborated with American students on innovative grassroots campaigns. She is the editor of SudanActivism.com.

JESSE SAGE
Jesse Sage is a board member of the American Anti-Slavery Group and for seven years was the organization's associate director. Founder of the web portal iAbolish.org, Sage has been recognized by *Fast Company* magazine as one of its "Fast 50" innovators. He is currently a program director for HAMSA and serves on the advisory board of the Committee to Protect Bloggers.

MICHELINE SLATTERY
Micheline Slattery was born to a prominent family in Haiti, but when tragedy left her orphaned at the age of five, she began her new life as a slave. For nine years, Slattery labored under the cruelty of her extended family, who routinely abused and degraded her. As a teenager, she was trafficked to Connecticut and continued to work as a slave until she was finally able to break free and begin a new life in the United States.

ABUK BAK
As a child of twelve, Abuk Bak was captured in a slave raid on her rural Southern Sudanese village. As her family was slaughtered by the Arab militia, Bak was dragged to the north and sold out of a slave pen "housing" other black Africans.

Bak spent the next ten years serving an Arab family as their shepherd and maid, finally escaping after a brutal rape attempt.

JILL LEIGHTON
A victim of sexual abuse at home and a runaway at fourteen, Jill Leighton was happy to find a sympathetic listener in a charming stranger named Bruce. Ignoring her instincts, she agreed to follow him home. So began three years of unimaginable sexual abuse and torture as Bruce prostituted the young teen as his slave.

BEATRICE FERNANDO
A native of Sri Lanka, Beatrice Fernando found herself enslaved in Lebanon after contracting with a job agency for a housemaid position. Forced to work as a domestic slave, Fernando endured months of brutal physical and emotional abuse. As a last resort, she jumped off her slaveholder's fourth-story balcony in an attempt to save her life and take back her freedom.

HARRY WU
A victim of Mao Zedong's oppressive policies, Harry Wu was labeled a "counterrevolutionary" and locked away in Chinese forced labor camps, known as *laogai*, for nineteen years. Wu draws from his experience of forced labor, torture, and severe illness to lobby against Chinese forced labor camps as the founder of the Laogai Research Foundation.

SELINA JUMA
In 2005, Selina Juma (name has been changed) accepted a position as an au pair through an Internet service, only to find herself held captive by her employers in Cairo, Egypt. Through covert e-mail correspondence with an American friend, Juma was able to employ the aid of international anti-slavery organizations and eventually extricate herself from bondage.

SVETA
Sveta (name has been changed) grew up in a poor Belarus town where big promises of wealth and glamour lured her to the city of Moscow and a life of sex slavery. Hardened by abuse, Sveta managed to escape from her slaveholders and, in a strange twist of fate, became a sex trafficker herself. Her testimony comes from a Belarus prison where she is currently being interned.

ABDEL NASSER OULD YESSA
As the son of a prominent political figure, Abdel Nasser Ould Yessa led a happy life in the northwestern African country of Mauritania. Inheriting Mauritania's chattel slavery system, in which Arab Berbers "own" black African slaves, Yessa didn't question societal norms until his encounter with a history book on the French Revolution taught him that all "men are born and remain free and equal in rights."

agreed to follow him home. So began three years of unimaginable sexual abuse and torture as Bruce prostituted the young teen as his slave.

BEATRICE FERNANDO

A native of Sri Lanka, Beatrice Fernando found herself enslaved in Lebanon after contracting with a job agency for a housemaid position. Forced to work as a domestic slave, Fernando endured months of brutal physical and emotional abuse. As a last resort, she jumped off her slaveholder's fourth-story balcony in an attempt to save her life and take back her freedom.

HARRY WU

A victim of Mao Zedong's oppressive policies, Harry Wu was labeled a "counter-revolutionary" and locked away in Chinese forced labor camps, known as *laogai*, for nineteen years. Wu draws from his experience of forced labor, torture, and severe illness to lobby against Chinese forced labor camps as the founder of the Laogai Research Foundation.

SELINA JUMA

In 2005, Selina Juma (name has been changed) accepted a position as an au pair through an Internet service, only to find herself held captive by her employers in Cairo, Egypt. Through covert e-mail correspondence with an American friend, Juma was able to employ the aid of international antislavery organizations and eventually extricate herself from bondage.

SVETA

Sveta (name has been changed) grew up in a poor Belarus town where big promises of wealth and glamour lured her to the city of Moscow and a life of sex slavery. Hardened by abuse, Sveta managed to escape from her slaveholders and, in a strange twist of fate, became a sex trafficker herself. Her testimony comes from a Belarus prison where she is currently being interned.

ABDEL NASSER OULD YESSA

As the son of a prominent political figure, Abdel Nasser Ould Yessa led a happy life in the northwestern African country of Mauritania. Inheriting Mauritania's chattel slavery system, in which Arab Berbers "own" black African slaves, Yessa didn't question societal norms until his encounter with a history book on the French Revolution taught him that all "men are born and remain free and equal in rights."

DISCUSSION GUIDE

1. Gloria Steinem begins her foreword with an epigraph: *"We must save the executioner from being the executioner as well as the victim from being the victim."* How did this affect the way you read each story in *Enslaved?*

2. How do the experiences of the women in *Enslaved* differ from those of the men? What do their experiences tell you about the relationship between women's rights and modern day slavery?

3. The slave narrative—a personal story written by a former slave—has been used as a political tool since the beginning of the abolitionist movement. What makes a personal story more powerful than, for example, a scholarly article? What are the risks involved in politicizing personal experiences? Are they worth it?

4. Consider other slave narratives, such as Harriet Jacobs' *Incidents in the Life of a Slave Girl* and *Narrative of the Life of Frederick Douglass, an American Slave.* How do the stories in *Enslaved* continue the tradition of the slave narrative? How do they deviate from it?

5. How did Salina Juma and Beatrice Fernando have their faith in God challenged and reinforced by their experiences of slavery? Is there anything surprising there?

6. Abdel Nasser Ould Yessa experienced a gradual awakening to the injustice of slavery. What does his story tell you about the challenges of eradicating slavery? How might they be overcome?

7. What is the significance of the title of chapter seven, "Atop the Second Wave"? How does Sveta's experience stand out? How did she continue to be a victim of trafficking even after becoming a trafficker herself?

8. Harry Wu writes, "Herein lies the essence of the Communist Party's art of governance, referred to as 'from the masses, to the masses' . . . They would lock you up or kill you, and still demand that you be utterly convinced and laud the decision loudly" (131). Harry Wu endured physical enslavement in the labor camps; here he describes a campaign of mental enslavement to go along with it. Talk about the relationship between physical and mental enslavement. What might this tell us about the strengths and weaknesses of the systems, institutions, or individuals that make modern day slavery possible?

9.   Jill Leighton's story is perhaps one of the most profoundly disturbing accounts in this volume; particularly troubling is the fact that, repeatedly, individuals who were in positions to help her did nothing. Why? What does that tell you about the importance of raising awareness?

10.   Are there any patterns to the stories of slavery in this book? What are they? What do they tell us about the roots of modern slavery and how it might be abolished?

For help, support and ideas on how you can take action, visit us online at http://www.iabolish.org/activist, or email us at enslaved@iabolish.org

"The only thing necessary for the triumph of evil is for good men to do nothing."

—*Edmund Burke*

CPSIA information can be obtained
at www.ICGtesting.com
Printed in the USA
LVHW040354081220
673560LV00004B/145

9 781403 974938